BEYOND HAMMER
BRITISH HORROR CINEMA SINCE 1970
BY
JAMES ROSE

auteur

First published in 2009 by
Auteur
The Old Surgery, 9 Pulford Road, Leighton Buzzard LU7 1AB
www.auteur.co.uk

Copyright © Auteur Publishing 2009

Designed and set by Nikki Hamlett at AMP Ltd, Dunstable, Bedfordshire

Printed and bound in Poland
www.polskabook.co.uk

Cover: *Shaun of The Dead* © Universal/Aquarius Collection

British Library Cataloguing-in-Publication Data
A catalogue record for this book is available from the British Library

ISBN 978-1-903663-97-4 (paperback)
ISBN 978-1-903663-98-1 (hardback)

CONTENTS

ACKNOWLEDGEMENTS

The author would like to thank John Atkinson at Auteur, for his sustained support and valued critique during the writing of this and many other critical texts. He would also like to thank Barry Rose for the many long telephone conversations about monsters, vampires and viruses. Thanks also to Helen Rose for all the proof reading and support as well as to family and friends for putting up with it all for the past 12 months.

The author and the publisher would like to thank Julian Richards for his assistance.

DEDICATIONS

This book is dedicated to Joan Lees and my English teachers Mrs. MacDonald and Mr. Davies.

AUTHOR'S NOTE

When writing a book about any period of cinema history, omissions have to be made. Be this due to space, time or relevance, some films that others would consider essential to such critiques are either briefly mentioned or left out entirely. Such is the case with this book. This is not due to those works being of a lesser quality than those included but more to the concept of the book itself: the intention is to present to student, tutor and the casual reader a sample of the depth and transitions evident with the history of the British horror film. As such films were selected that would explore specific moments, qualities and readings in order to provide a chronology of this often maligned part of British cinema.

A version of chapter 10 (*The Descent*) first appeared in *Splice*, Volume 2 issue 1 (autumn 2007).

INTRODUCTION

Dominating British horror cinema is, perhaps predictably, Hammer Studios: in 1968, the studio was honoured with the Queen's Award for Industry in recognition for the role they had so far played in raising the profile of British cinema on both a national and international scale. Five years later and the golden age of Hammer would be over, taking with it the last vestiges of the Great British Horror Film whilst the rest of the British film industry struggled with minimal state funding and the withdrawal of American financing. Through her analysis of the era, Sarah Street notes that apart from the lack of financial support, 'cinema admissions were declining at the same time as the popularity of television and other amusements increased, a trend the arrival of multiplexes in the mid-1970s could not reverse' (1997: 93). From here the British film industry, one that had flourished both critically and commercially only a decade earlier, began its steady decline whilst attempting to reconstruct itself through the period / costume dramas before shifting its concerns into more contemporary narratives.

THE PAST

Hammer's output is often considered as a unique body of film production, one marked by the *auteurist* stamp not of the director but of the studio itself: the historic location that is drenched in Gothic signifiers, mist shrouded landscapes, period costumes, heroic males and monstrous women all presided over by the classic literary manifestations of Count Dracula and Victor Frankenstein. So bound to these motifs, Hammer is synonymous with renderings of the Gothic to the extent that its contextual and conceptual concerns are sometimes lost and often overlooked.

In her brief chronology of Hammer's output of this era, Street notes that 'in the 1960s there were significant developments which drew on conventions established by Hammer yet at the same time incorporated new stylistic trends and reflected contemporary anxieties' (ibid.). These anxieties were predominately focused on an increasing sense of male insecurity and its manifestation through the abuse of the independent woman[1]. Such concerns were rising out of a British society where women were establishing themselves within the nation's work force, simultaneously fragmenting the established family order and undermining the perceived masculine role as the family's prime income generator. Horror, with its dominating male heroes and its weak female victims, became an ideal platform within which to express these concerns, a situation made all the more contentious as the censorship system relaxed enough to allow for an increase in nudity and scenes of sexual intimacy.

ORIGINS

Although the emergence of cultural concerns and anxieties is blatantly evident in

Hammer's declining years, it is also present at its very start: in its earliest days, Hammer's film production lay predominately with low budget thrillers coupled with adaptations of British television and radio programmes. Although popular enough to recoup the budgetary costs, the studio had yet to achieve considerable national and international success. In an effort to gain such recognition, executives James Carreras and Anthony Hinds purchased the film rights to the BBC's groundbreaking serial *The Quatermass Experiment* (1953).

Written by Nigel Kneale, the series concerned the premature return to Earth of Professor Bernard Quatermass's experimental manned rocket. Having sealed off the crash site, Quatermass soon learns that only one of the three astronauts, Carroon, has survived. Whilst under Quatermass's care, it becomes apparent that Carroon is both severely traumatised and possibly infected with an extra-terrestrial disease. Whilst Quatermass tries to establish what has happened to the other two astronauts, Carroon escapes his hospital confines and begins, against his will, a slow and painful mutation into a space creature, killing anyone who crosses his path.

Kneale's original television series and Hammer's subsequent adaptation are both preoccupied with the notion of invasion. As a popular genre of American cinema in the fifties, the science fiction invasion film functioned as that nation's fear of the Communist threat, constructing the alien as a political and social force that would both invade and absorb the minds of its men, women and children. As a consequence, many of these films have a severe paranoia running through them, a quality most evident in *Invasion of the Body Snatchers* (Don Siegel, 1956). For Kneale the monster is not necessarily Communism and is one that is not immediately a threat to the British nation, instead he chooses to focus on the plight of one man's contamination as a means of expressing the potential fate of a populace. In this respect, readings of both the television series and the film adaptation suggest not just the terrors of a possible Cold War but more a reflection on Britain in a post-World War era: 'Newman states that unlike their American counterparts, British science fiction invasion films of the 1950's seem to be "still fighting World War 2'" (Hutchings, 1999: 38). This is evidently true of *Quatermass* where the imagery and landscape recall a war torn country, imagery which is most blatantly manifested in the film's opening

> '… in which a rocket crashes near a cottage in the country, neatly dramatis[ing] a much more widespread collision that takes place throughout this and the other *Quatermass* narratives between the fantastic regime of science fiction and the 'realism' of British everyday life.' (Hutchings, 1999: 38)

Kneale perhaps consciously considered this contextual possibility when writing the serial for he has stated in interview:

> 'I wanted to write some strong characters, but I didn't want them to be like those horrible people in those awful American science fiction films, chewing gum and stating the obvious.

Not that I wanted to do something terribly "British", but I really didn't like all the flag-waving
you got in those films.' (Wells, 1999: 50)

With such comments, Kneale's *Quatermass* serial and screenwriter Richard Landau's
subsequent film adaptation are predictably bleak in their content and pessimistic in their
outlook: some of the characters die painful deaths whilst others manage to survive the horror
but remain physically, mentally and emotionally traumatised by their experience, an apt and
appropriate analogy for those that experienced the war both on the front and at home.

In order to ensure a solid commercial success, Carreras requested that Landau and
director Val Guest expand upon the narrative's horrific elements in order to gain the film
an X (Adults Only) Certificate. Carreras would then exploit the emphasis upon this by
deliberately misspelling the film's title. This seemed a viable strategy, particularly given that
the adaptation process would involve reducing the three hour serial into a 90 minute film
and so allow for more emphasis to be placed on Carroon's grotesque mutation.

All of this worked as Carreras had planned and the BBFC awarded *The Quatermass
Xperiment* (1955) the desired X Certificate, making it one of the first British films to
receive that certification. During its initial release the film generated large audience
figures in Britain and then went onto the US to repeat similar business, making
Quatermass Hammer's first international success.

THE MONSTER

When adapting *Quatermass*, Guest wisely balanced the graphic horror of the
transformation with the tragedy of Carroon's absorption, rendering the character in a
similar manner to Frankenstein's creation – mute and grotesque but painfully human.
Although clearly representing the narrative's manifestation of evil, Carroon embodies a
very strong sense of innocence: he is not fundamentally evil but more a *construct* of evil.
This sense of constructed evil manifests itself throughout the British horror film, be that
through an extra-terrestrial infection as in *Quatermass*, through religious belief as in *The
Wicker Man* (Robin Hardy, 1973) or simply through their very creation as in *Mary Shelley's
Frankenstein* (Kenneth Branagh, 1994) and results in monsters that are not supernatural
creatures but perversions of rational humanity. Because of this quality, the majority
of British monsters are provided the opportunity to speak: through this dialogue the
monster is allowed to express themselves, to communicate their thoughts and feelings
and, at times, to respond to their condition and comment upon it, a quality most evident
in Clive Barker's *Hellraiser* (1987) and Julian Richard's *The Last Horror Movie* (2003). This
self reflective nature encourages a certain sense of audience sympathy with some of
these monsters (Carroon, Frankenstein's creation and Carmilla in Roy Ward Baker's *The
Vampire Lovers* [1970]) as the narrative and dialogue force the viewer into considering
the emotional values of the monster. As a result, the majority of the films explored in this
book suggest the focus is not on the supernatural monster but the *human* monster.

7

REALISM

Guest chose to shoot *The Quatermass Xperiment* in black and white and, wherever he could, with a hand-held camera, in order to create a documentary feel. This emphasised the realist qualities of the narrative and, in a tangential way, pre-empts the emergence of the national cinema's preoccupation with social realism in the emerging 'Kitchen Sink' dramas of the following decade. Carroon's horrific plight is made all the more poignant through this cinematic mode as the unsteady camera follows him through the post-war landscape of London, down past canals and back out into the streets where his mutation completes its cycle at Westminster Abbey. Shooting on location, the reality is again heightened and increases the horrific values for the then contemporary audience: having just survived a war, they could make strong emotional connections between the rocket crashing and the seemingly desolate spaces in which Carroon stumbles through. To a certain extent this played upon certain negative feeling within society, but the decision (made by the original writer, Kneale) to conclude the film at Westminster Abbey brings a more positive feeling to the film because the coronation of the Queen had taken place there three months prior to the release of the film and so, as a tangible space within the capital city, the Abbey operated as a site of new beginnings for post-war Britain. Although the monster manifests itself there and presents its threat to this symbol of New Britain, it is, of course, also killed there, leaving the building unscarred and intact, a symbol of hope and a bright, new future.

The use of a realist mode within subsequent British horror is evident in the majority of works, including *Hellraiser, 28 Days Later* (Danny Boyle, 2002) *The Last Horror Movie* and, more recently, in Neil Marshall's *The Descent* (2005). Each film uses the mode in a different way in an effort to specifically place the horrific into the public and private spaces of the British landscape and its culture. Once established within those spaces, the monstrous elements reconfigure the landscape and transform them primarily into hunting grounds (such as with the London Underground in *Death Line* [Gary Sherman, 1972], *An American Werewolf in London* [John Landis, 1981] and *Creep* [Christopher Smith, 2004]) whereas others, such as *28 Days Later* and *Shaun of the Dead* (Edgar Wright, 2004), position their protagonists in overly familiar landscapes that are then subverted through catastrophic incident.

REFLECTING THE TIMES

One of the most significant qualities of *Quatermass* is its contextual reading as a reflector of the times. As previously mentioned, both the original serial and film were released at a time when the country was steadily rebuilding itself physically and emotionally from war. The imagery of a foreign invader would have been quite a potent symbol and one which would make manifest old fears and anxieties. The idea to make the invader extra-terrestrial serves a two-fold purpose: initially it distances the value of the threat from any explicit, real world threats yet its origin as a space creature tapped directly into a different public anxiety, that of the escalating space race between East and West. When *Quatermass* was released, the British manned space programme was in its infancy but fears of what was 'out there' were aroused within the public who now feared a different type of invader than the Nazis. This was coupled with the development of the V2 bomb (Quatermass has named his rocket Q2) and the public's knowledge that Britain had being launching its first guided missiles. Although the war was over, new threats were appearing in the shadows of space and Britain was arming itself, making preparations for perhaps a far bigger and more violent enemy.

The majority of the films analysed within this book share this essential trait: first and foremost they exist to entertain by terrifying their audience but on a deeper level they are written as a response to the era in which the writer and film-maker are living: *The Vampire Lovers* blatantly communicates a fear of the emergent independent woman whilst *The Descent* explores the emotional collapse and consequential regression of one such woman; *The Wicker Man* critiques a society that embraces freedom and sexual liberation through its very opposite, the repressed Christian; whilst *Death Line* suggests an examination of societal ignorance towards the poor and the impoverished. Others embrace events specific to the country whilst associating it with more global concerns as do writer Alex Garland and director Danny Boyle in *28 Days Later* who use a fictional virus to comment upon the BSE crisis and AIDS epidemic while Branagh's *Mary Shelley's Frankenstein* reconfigures the classic Gothic text for an age of cloning and IVF reproduction. The remainder are there to purely entertain, yet there are subtle metaphors that correlate to other examples of the genre or reference the directors' personal concerns and responses to the world that surrounds them.

It is evident that from these essential qualities that *Quatermass* has the potential to be positioned as perhaps the archetypal British horror film for it defined an influential set of parameters by which a national cinema could make a genre film. Its representations of the Monster, sense of realism and contextual values all reverberate through the subsequent eras of British horror and suggest that such genre films form an important part of the British cultural identity as much as its national cinema's identity. With such a heritage it seems a contradiction then to acknowledge the distinct lack of genre cinema emerging from Britain after the slow and steady collapse of Hammer Studios: *To The Devil a Daughter* (Peter Sykes, 1976) would be Hammer's last horror film and suggested to many not just the end of an era but also the death of the Great British horror film itself.

ENDNOTES

[1] See Chapter 1: *The Vampire Lovers* as a prime example of this.

REFERENCES

Hutchings, Peter. "'We're the Martians now'": British sf invasion fantasies of the 1950s and 1960s' in Hunter, I. Q. (ed.) *British Science Fiction Cinema*, London: Routledge, 1999.

Street, Sarah. *British National Cinema*, London: Routledge, 1997.

Wells, Paul. 'Apocalypse then! The ultimate monstrosity and strange things on the coast… an interview with Nigel Kneale' in Hunter, I. Q. (ed.) *British Science Fiction Cinema*, London: Routledge, 1999.

CHAPTER I: THE VAMPIRE LOVERS

'As the 1970s dawned, the British film industry was in crisis mode yet again, only this time it would prove terminal. The American majors, who… throughout the latter part of the 1960s had lavished money on British production, were registering massive financial losses at home and accordingly withdrew their support.' (Rigby, 2002: 196)

At the turn of the decade the British Board of Film Censors began to redress the boundaries of the censorship system. As a consequence, Secretary John Trevelyan increased the entry age for an X certificate to 18 years and at the same time introduced a new certificate, the AA, whose lower age limit was 14 years. Instead of seeing this change as detrimental to film production, British studios, executives, writers and directors saw it as an opportunity to increase the graphic content of their films. The revised X became an opportunity to depict stronger acts of violence, to show more nudity and to depict with more clarity sexual contact and the sex act itself. As a consequence, 'British horror films were now progressing to exploitative details which would have been unimaginable only five years before. Hammer led the way with a film which was emblematic not only of the relaxed censorship but also of the American desertion of Britain's sinking studios' (Rigby, 2002: 197). That film was *The Vampire Lovers* (Roy Ward Baker, 1970).

As if to make their exploitative intentions blatantly clear, screenwriter Tudor Gates and director Roy Ward Baker, opened their film by deceiving the audience into believing they are watching another classic Hammer vampire film: a shrouded figure drifts out of a fog-wreathed graveyard. As this entity floats forward it slowly transforms into a woman in a diaphanous gown. She heads towards the remains of a castle where a man, Baron Joachim von Hartog (Douglas Wilmer), waits. They embrace – and here is where the break with Hammer tradition is first signalled. As they embrace the woman's ample cleavage crushes against the Baron's crucifix (Fig. 1). She screams as the metal burns into her flesh, her lips pulling back to reveal her fangs. She lunges for the Baron's throat but he is quick and, drawing his sword, he swiftly decapitates her with a single stroke of his blade.

Fig. 1: Cleavage and the Cross

This brief but violent death draws together three potent images – the crucifix, breasts and decapitation – into one powerful sequence that is simultaneously seductive, erotic and ugly. In this one vampire's death, Baker coherently encapsulates Hammers new approach to horror and by doing so marked the beginning of the studio's steady decline into exploitation territory.

This opening deception is two-fold. Not only does it function as this marker in the shift in tone from classic horror to exploitation, it also marks a considerable generic shift in the power of the vampire. Up until the release of *The Vampire Lovers*, the majority of cinematic vampires were constructed around a series of established rules: as unholy creatures they fear both sunlight and the symbolic power of the Cross, they drink the blood of the innocent, and can be killed either by a stake through the heart or through decapitation. Baker's opening sequence draws all of these facets again into one and so suggests to the audience that the vampires of this film are going to be within a traditional mode. But, as the narrative unfolds, it soon becomes apparent that these vampires are far from those of the established cinematic mode.

ORIGINS: THE VAMPIRE

Since its first appearance in F. W. Murnau's *Nosferatu* (1922), the vampire has enjoyed a sustained cinematic profile. The reason for this is, as Odell and Le Blanc suggest in their book *Vampire Cinema*, that as a symbol the vampire can be successfully 'reinvented and rediscovered by each generation to mirror their fears and desires' (2000: 7). It is the vampire's very mutability as a symbol that sustains it: Murnau's *Nosferatu* can be read as a metaphorical reflection of 'the prevalent anti-Semitic attitudes of Weimar Germany or… perhaps the vampire's abject and terrifying qualities mirrored Murnau's sense of ostracism as a gay man in that place and time' (Goldberg, 2007: 168). Seventy years later, Francis Ford Coppola's *Bram Stoker's Dracula* (1992) and Neil Jordan's *Interview with a Vampire*

(1994) can both be read as texts preoccupied with sexuality and the emergence of HIV. In these two films the narrative implied (as it does in Murnau's film) that vampirism is a disease, an illness resulting from a blood borne virus. Other vampire films suggest other readings, as Odell and Le Blanc observe. *Vamp* (Richard Wenk, 1986) concerns a sexually predatory female (and so reflects the emergence of the strong and independent female, picturing it as a threat to the dominant patriarchy) whilst other vampire films deftly fuse genres to make their commentary – John Badham's adaptation of *Dracula* (1979) is an infusion of the romantic bodice ripper with horror whilst Kathryn Bigelow's *Near Dark* (1987) merges the vampire with the Western to explore contemporary representations of the family unit.

This diversity of readings constructs an index of repeated symbolic values or concerns within the figure of the vampire. Odell and Le Blanc (2000) suggest that the following four values are all indicative within a vampire film. Sometimes only one factor may appear but, for the most part, two or three of the factors work in unison in order to create the anticipated meaning:

1) Aristocracy

The origins of the vampire myth lie not in literature but in folklore, specifically in stories from Eastern Europe. As Punter and Byron state, in these stories the vampire was 'little more than a shambling and mindless creature [who] was of peasant stock, preyed on his or her immediate family or neighbours, and functioned primarily to explain the spread of disease and sudden deaths in the community' (2003: 268). From these beginnings the vampire myth developed in depth and dimension with each successive interpretation. One of the most significant aspects of this development was the vampire's shift from oral folklore to written literature – in myth the vampire was merely a disease-ridden peasant but when they began to appear in literature they rapidly escalated through the social order and assumed aristocratic position.

As Goldberg's reading of *Nosferatu* suggests, the aristocratic nature of the vampire implies a significant range of interpretations in relation to society and its inherent class systems: as a representation, the upper class vampire preys upon the poor working classes, literally draining the life from them. If he chooses to let them live then they become his subordinate, another servant within their horrific household. This social status and its associated connotations reverberate through the remainder of the vampire legacy, a factor most evident in *Interview with a Vampire* where Odell and Le Blanc describe the vampire Lestat (Tom Cruise) as the 'snob who loved to hunt in society' (2000: 85).

2) Sexuality

As a member of the aristocracy, Count Dracula is an embodiment of wealth, charm, elegance and opulence. From these qualities emerges the clichéd fantasy of the handsome prince who falls in love with the pauper girl. With just one special kiss, this poor girl can leave behind a lifetime of poverty and enter into the rich freedom of the upper classes. Because of this, the Count is, without doubt, one of the most sexually charged manifestations within horror cinema, especially as depicted by Hammer and Christopher Lee: with his hypnotic stare, Dracula is presented as the arch seducer who appears before virgin maidens in the midnight hour, drawing them into the folds of his red lined cape where his kiss becomes a bite and his love becomes contagious. Through this inherent sexuality, the vampire represents a release from sexual repression and becomes a metaphor for sex, sexuality and, at times, sexual deviance. In this symbolic mode, Dracula can be read as a female fantasy figure for he is a sort of Prince Charming, the 'other man' whose sexual acts are both desired and forbidden. With the vampire, sexual intercourse is not physically necessary, for congress is played out through the penetration of the female's neck – the piercing fangs become phallic, the drinking and exchanging of blood both sexual and contaminating, the perfect symbol for the desired and the forbidden.

3) Disease

The gaining of this forbidden desire comes at a significant price as, in all their manifestations, whether it is in literature or on screen, the vampire is visually and metaphorically contextualised as a disease. In Murnau's *Nosferatu*, the titular vampire appears surrounded by a swarm of rats, suggesting that this creature is the embodiment of the plague; whilst more contemporary interpretations, such as in Coppola's adaptation, vampirism is equated with AIDS through intimate images of vampiric blood entering into uninfected bloodstreams. The blood borne nature of vampirism is central to the consistent reconfiguration of the vampire's meaning, making this symbol plastic in terms of cultural representation. Although the majority of these connotations are negative, some films, such as *The Hunger* (Tony Scott, 1983) and *The Lost Boys* (Joel Schumacher, 1987), suggest that the disease can also be perceived as a positive force: vampirism reconfigures the biology of the host to allow for immortality, a seemingly endless life of power, wealth and decadence. As the tag line for *The Lost Boys* states: 'Sleep all day. Party all night. Never grow old. Never die. It's fun to be a vampire.'

A further reading of this connotation is that the figure of the vampire suggests an anxiety regarding the loss of identity: '…as the victim is changed into a vampire… he/she looses a sense of self and becomes the very thing that had attacked him/her, obliterating any difference between them' (Paul, 1994: 388). This reading of the vampire correlates the nature of the vampiric contamination with those films preoccupied with the paranoia of disease – most notably Danny Boyle's *28 Days Later* where the Rage virus is communicable by blood and transforms its hosts into a mass of mindless, bloodthirsty psychopaths.

4) The Fear of Growing Old

Approaching vampirism as a positive disease suggests a further metaphoric value of the vampire – their immortality cancels out our own mortality and so quells fears and anxieties relating to our own deaths. Death is inevitable yet the vampire – and their disease – offers an alternative. In *The Lost Boys* and *Near Dark*, the young protagonists are seduced by such a possibility, even more so by the fact that when one is bitten they remain fixed within that age, living their life as an eternal youth where they will never grow old (and so never have to face the responsibilities of adulthood) nor will they ever die (suggesting a lifetime free of illness and, ironically, terminal disease). But, as each narrative unfolds, it soon becomes apparent that eternal life is not as seductive as it first seems with each of the young protagonists turning to murder in order to sustain their immortality.

The Hunger and *Interview with a Vampire* consider this facet of vampirism by examining the horror and the loneliness as the price of immortality. *The Hunger* takes this concept as its central premise: 'More than anything, what the film embodies is a fear of death and aging. Rarely has the sense of the creeping obscenity of age eating away at beauty and the sense of powerlessness it brings been conveyed' (Scheib, 2008). *Interview with a Vampire* approaches this concern from the notion of the family – Louis (Brad Pitt) wants a child so Lestat finds him a young girl, Claudia (Kristen Dunst) and turns her. For a while this aberrant family unit functions but as Claudia stays fixed in the body of five year old, her mind develops into adulthood and so desires what most adults wish for – a partner and a sexual relationship. This, of course, creates readings of the endless child and, more perversely, the child as lover.

ORIGINS: CARMILLA

Aberrant sexuality is not uncommon in vampiric texts. In his readings of Bram Stoker's novel *Dracula*, Robin Wood suggests that the Count connotes an image of bisexuality as much as an image of heterosexual desire (1996: 370–1). This and similar readings are constructed from the vampire's choice of victim in relation to the phallic nature of biting and drinking blood from their victim's neck. Rarely does a vampire feed solely upon the opposite sex and so combined with the aforementioned sexual connotations, this does suggest a bisexual quality to virtually all vampires. It is important to stress that this quality is often suppressed and merely hinted at within both written and visual texts, yet there are some texts which openly engage with this idea. One of the first and perhaps one of the most influential was Joseph Sheridan Le Fanu's *Carmilla*.

Published in 1872, Le Fanu's gothic novella predates Stoker's *Dracula* by 25 years. It was first published in three parts in *The Dark Blue* magazine and was later published in the same year as a novella in a collection of the author's stories, *In a Glass Darkly* (1872). The narrative concerns the arrival of a Countess's daughter, Carmilla Karnstein, into the home of the Morton family. Carmilla and Laura Morton soon become friends but it becomes apparent that Carmilla seems to have a particular and unusual attraction to Laura and a tendency to sleep until late in the afternoon. Soon Laura becomes ill and her father takes to the deserted village of Karnstein. There they encounter General Spielsdorf who reveals that Carmilla is an age-old vampire. The story concludes with Carmilla's grave exhumed and her body appropriately destroyed.

In an anonymous introduction to a 1995 printing of *In a Glass Darkly*, *Carmilla* is described as being:

> '…a curious mixture of traditional vampire-lore and Irish folklore. The beautiful vampire Carmilla has much in common with traditional Irish female spirits, who were often attached to a particular family, though her strong sexuality is a characteristic vampire attribute. Le Fanu overtly uses lesbianism, which was not only a taboo subject at the time but which had all sorts of evil connotations, to heighten tension and to symbolise abnormality'. (Le Fanu, 1995: x)

Le Fanu did not shy away from the homoerotic relationship Carmilla engenders nor the revulsion at her homosexuality, dealing with it appropriately for the era in which he wrote:

> 'She used to place her pretty arms about my neck, draw me to her, and laying her cheek to mine, murmur with her lips near my ear… And when she had spoken such a rhapsody, she would press me more closely in her trembling embrace, and her lips in soft kisses gently glow upon my cheek… Her murmured words sounded like a lullaby in my ear, and soothed my resistance into a trance, from which I only seemed to recover myself when she withdrew her arms… I experienced a strange tumultuous excitement that was pleasurable but was ever and anon mingled with a vague sense of fear and disgust.' (Le Fanu, 1995: 225)

Such was the success and endurance of the Le Fanu novella that *Carmilla* became the basis for a number of lesbian vampire films. In her essay *Daughters of Darkness*, Bonnie Zimmerman suggests that Carl Dreyer's *Vampyr* (1932) is a loose adaptation of *Carmilla*, albeit one free of any suggestion of lesbian sexuality. Zimmerman also identifies *Dracula's Daughter* (Lambert Hillyer, 1936), *The Blood of Dracula* (Herbert L. Strock, 1957), *Et Mourir de Plaisir* (*Blood and Roses* [Roger Vadim, 1960]) and *La Maldicion de los Karnstein* (*Terror in the Crypt* [Camillo Mastrocinque, 1964]) as being in this tradition (1996: 379–80).

In narrative terms, Tudor Gates' adaptation, *The Vampire Lovers*, actually keeps remarkably close to the original text. The only significant differences are a restructuring of events, the introduction of a new character – Baron Hartog – and, more importantly, allowing Carmilla to seduce and feed upon men as well as women. In the novella, Carmilla's seductions and attacks are solely upon women, making even more explicit the homosexual connotations of the text.

CARMILLA'S ARISTOCRACY

Carmilla's aristocratic background is an essential part of the film's narrative for she is the last surviving member of a vampire family, the Karnsteins. With the rest of her family murdered by Baron Hartog, Carmilla lives undead as an orphan, a wraith that drifts from wealthy surrogate family to wealthy surrogate family in order to both feed and, perversely, to feel a sense of belonging.

Fig. 2: Carmilla the aristocrat

It would seem at first that *The Vampire Lovers* subverts the vampire's choice of victim by allowing Carmilla (Ingrid Pitt) to prey only upon the rich blood aristocracy but as the film progresses the narrative is broken up by singular scenes in which Carmilla attacks and feeds upon peasant women. The first is wandering alone through the woods whilst the second is attacked whilst she sleeps. Her assaults upon these women first reflect Carmilla's brutality as she chases the woman before pouncing upon her, whilst the second attack is rendered more as a seduction than as an assault: the woman lies asleep in her bed as (in reference to Murnau's *Nosferatu*) the shadow of Carmilla's arm and hand reaches across the wall. As her hand comes into the frame the woman wakes but before she can scream her gaze relaxes as if she were mesmerised. Carmilla touches the woman's lips in a sensual manner, lightly tracing their outline. Director Baker then cuts to an exterior shot of the woman's home. There is a brief pause and then a scream. These brief attacks subtly suggest a sense of frustration on Carmilla's part: she cannot have the love and lives of those she desires so in frustrated rage, Carmilla hunts those she knows she *can* have – the poor.

In terms of representation the wealthy are, perhaps predictably, depicted as a clean and restrained group of people. The opening birthday party scene constructs the parameters of this social group through the opulence of the room – numerous chandeliers, scarlet drapes and oil paintings that are large enough to fill the wall. The room's finery is matched by its guests, who all wear formal dress: neat and trimmed they dance as servants wait upon their needs. At the centre of all this is General Spielsdorf (Peter Cushing). He stands tall and upright in his bright red uniform, his many medals catching the glow of the candles. As he watches his guests he appears very much like Carmilla will when she first enters this scene, attractive and powerful but distanced from those within the room. His presence here indicates wealth, dominance and patriarchal control.

As the scene evolves other men are depicted in a similar manner, with each appearing to be wealthy and holding some sense of status within their peer group. Their accompanying partners are also depicted as being of wealthy stock with their tight dresses and sparkling jewellery highlighting each woman's beauty. As the narrative progresses, the aristocratic males position as the dominant force is made all the more obvious yet the women's roles are reduced to those of naïve young women in desperate need of masculine protection: Emma (Madeline Smith) and Laura (Pippa Steele) are both depicted as being weak and frail even before Carmilla begins her seductions and vampiric feeding, with both being lost in romantic daydreaming as they long for a boyfriend. This sense of immaturity contrasts sharply with Carmilla's world-weary approach to life. Here she is the dominant one, working her way into the family unit in order to slake her thirst for aristocratic blood.

It is worth noting that for a narrative that is preoccupied with the invasion of the family, there are no mothers nor is there any mention of where Emma or Laura's mothers are, or even if they are alive or dead. Instead, Laura is being looked after by her grandfather, The General, whilst Emma lives at home with her father (George Cole) and a Governess. As a surrogate mother, the Governess (Kate O'Mara) is at first shown to be a strong and determined woman but she too soon succumbs to Carmilla's seductions.

Although it remains below the surface of the film, *The Vampire Lovers* somewhat alarmingly suggests that all women are weak and in need of patriarchal protection whilst simultaneously suggesting that women who are strong (and the only female that represents this is Carmilla) are aberrant and need to be suppressed by the dominant patriarchy.

CARMILLA'S SEXUALITY

Part of the reason for the emergence of the British sex-vampire film at this time was an aberration within the British censorship system: a film could depict nudity and sexual acts as long as it was framed within the context of a fantasy narrative. The vampire, with their inherent connection to sex, must have seemed to studio executives the ideal vehicle through which a director could legitimately indulge and satisfy the audience with prolonged imagery of female nudity. Although this may seem a blunt way to engage the audience's prurience (and, as has been already seen with *The Quatermass Xperiment*, Hammer was not averse to using the censorship system to gain its audience), these films, consciously or not, generated images that would broaden readings of the vampire more widely and, as a consequence, deviate its natural development as the emphasis shifted from the dominating masculine vampire to the female vampire seductress. As David Pirie states:

> '…with the new sex-vampire movies, attention moved almost exclusively over to the woman… In literal social terms this was of course the most reactionary stereotype available, and to make matters worse it was proliferating at precisely the time when the distorting cultural image of women was coming under deserved criticism. A good many people, perhaps discovering the vampire movie for the first time, attacked it as degrading and sexist.' (1977: 99)

Although Pirie agrees with these criticisms, he also suggests that the Vampire is an incarnation of 'the most hostile aspects of sexuality in a concrete form' (ibid.). This, to a certain extent, only adds further weight to negative criticism of such films but it also suggests a peculiarly resonant support of the changing image of women. Within *The Vampire Lovers* women are shown to be both weak *and* strong, naïve *and* dominant. The weak are seduced by the strong lesbian vampire Carmilla. Her seductions are gentle and without violence as she coaxes her potential lovers into embracing their own latent homosexuality to the extent that sexual contact and consequential blood sucking are both desired and accepted by the victim. Because of these consensual seductions, Carmilla's gender and sexual orientation are a blatant undermining of patriarchal society – the very society that created the 'distorting cultural image of women'. In this respect Carmilla is depicted as a woman who knows what she wants and understands how to get it. It comes then as no surprise that the film ends with a group of patriarchs – Baron Hartog and General Spielsdorf – hunting Carmilla down to impale her with their sharpened phallic stakes. As if this is not enough, they proceed to behead her[1] (Fig. 3 and 4, below).

Perversely, this ending consolidates the emergence of the strong, independent woman: in *The Vampire Lovers* such a woman is to be feared and must therefore be killed by the masculine; yet the fear she generates is felt exclusively by males. Carmilla only poses a threat to the patriarchal society whereas her seductions allow her female victims to explore and express aspects of their identity that had so far been oppressed by the patriarch.

For all the queer readings of this vampire, Carmilla's death operates on an ambiguous level. Odell and Le Blanc comment that her decapitation 'has been seen by some writers as punishment for her lesbianism' but then quite rightly point out that this 'is really no different to the fate of any screen vampire – they are punished for the threat they pose to 'decent' society, regardless of sexual orientation' (2000: 25). Herein lies the uncertainty and so suggests that the viewer has to decide for themselves as to whether Carmilla is killed for sinning against mankind or for sinning against the sexual norms of established patriarchy.

CARMILLA'S DISEASE

For all its conventional, if fashionably explicit, sexuality and violence, *The Vampire Lovers* actually presents a revisionist approach to the vampire: although the narrative depicts Carmilla as monstrous, the dialogue constructs her as a sad and lonely creature. Whereas most vampires have a yearning for blood, Carmilla desires that which she cannot have – affection and the possibility of love. Although beautiful, Carmilla is a vampire, the Other, the one who is not part of normal society. When she first appears at Laura's birthday party, she is wearing a vivid red dress, her necklace a single red ruby, hanging like a drop

of blood against her cleavage (Fig. 5). Her beauty attracts the attention of the majority of the men in the room yet Carmilla stands apart from them, quietly observing as the guests dance or talk. She is literally on the periphery and, although it is of course possible she is merely looking for prey, there is a certain sadness in this scene.

Fig. 5: Carmilla's blood-like jewellery

While everyone else enjoys their normal lives, Carmilla must stand at the very edges, forever knowing that she cannot be part of this normal society, looking not for victims but for acceptance and love.

As if to underline this, Carmilla is suddenly approached by a number of men, all reaching out to take her hand, to kiss her and ask for a dance. It seems as if one lucky man is granted his wish and Carmilla accompanies him to the dance floor. There they dance but instead of looking at her potential suitor, Carmilla's gaze remains fixed on Laura and *her* partner, Carl. Laura notices and suggests to Carl that Carmilla wants to take him away from her. Carl looks across at Carmilla and replies, 'Nonsense, she's looking at you'. Although seemingly 'embraced' by the normal, patriarchal society through her acceptance of the dance, Carmilla remains fixated upon Laura, still observing that which she cannot, according to that 'normal' society, have.

The first indication of Carmilla's sexuality is signified here but it doesn't quite manifest itself within Carmilla's and Laura's subsequent relationship. Although it is obvious that Carmilla is attracted to Laura, it soon becomes apparent that she does not love her and instead uses her to feed upon and for (it is assumed) sexual gratification: when Carmilla feeds upon Laura, she sucks the blood from her breast. As she does so, Laura experiences 'nightmare dreams' that are visualised as surrealistic and sexually charged moments. Presented in black and white, each nightmare is a montage of images, each slightly blurred and overlaid with the next. Whilst Laura writhes in her bed, the eyes of a black cat fill the screen which, in turn, is super-imposed over Carmilla's eyes. A mass of fur then creeps up the bed towards Laura as her movements become more panicked. There are more images of cats' eyes and rapid cutting back and forth between this and Carmilla's face before Laura finally wakes up screaming. Whilst the incident is certainly upsetting for

Laura (and so could certainly be read as a form of rape), it is gratifying for Carmilla for she slakes both her lust for blood and sexual intimacy with another female (Fig. 6).

This nightmare imagery is sustained when Carmilla begins her seduction of Emma. Like Laura she soon falls under Carmilla's spell and becomes both an unwilling lover

Fig. 6: The female vampire as seductress

as much as a source of nourishment. For all her assaults on Emma, it becomes apparent that Carmilla is genuinely attracted to her and seemingly falls in love with her. And, even though she expresses this attraction verbally, Emma, in her innocence, misunderstands these gestures. It is here that Carmilla's true sadness comes to the fore. 'I want you to love me for all your life', says Carmilla knowing full well that this may never happen. Perhaps it is here that the vampire manifests the fear of old age, the terror of staying forever young whilst those around you grow old and whither into death.

Consequently, *The Vampire Lovers* represents vampirism as a disease that is resented as much by the carrier as it is feared by the superstitious: throughout the course of the film, Carmilla's status as a vampire is signified as much as a curse than anything else, forever trapping her in an ageless body but denying that she spend eternity with any of those that she loves. She becomes a tragic figure whose melancholy is clearly expressed when she discusses death with Emma. Having witnessed the funeral parade of one of her victims, Carmilla screams in anger. Emma calms her and asks why she is so upset, to which Carmilla explains that she despises death for it takes people away from her. This is obviously ironic for she herself is the harbinger of death yet her very awareness of it sets her apart from other depictions of vampires, particularly those of previous Hammer films where Dracula, played by the ubiquitous Christopher Lee, positively thrives upon the death and destruction he brings. Carmilla's self awareness enforces the idea of her as being cursed by her very nature and, possibly, by her homosexuality. Her vampiric state forces her into actions she does not wish to carry out yet are essential to her survival. This, in turn, constructs Carmilla as a duality of unwanted oppositions: a murderer and a confused lover.

As the narrative draws to a close, Carmilla's attempts to secure a future with Emma take increasingly desperate measures: she seduces the Governess, then murders the doctor before she transgresses her sexual preferences and seduces (and presumably murders) the butler, Renton. Having done this, Carmilla tries to get Emma to leave the house but the Governess intervenes. But, instead of trying to stop Carmilla, she begs her to take her with her. Carmilla responds by feeding upon her one more time, killing her in the process. This final vampiric act is witnessed by Emma who now, no longer naïve, sees Carmilla's true nature and screams in terror. Their relationship, now exposed, is rejected and once more Carmilla must kill that which she loves the most in order for her to survive. Perhaps it comes as no surprise then that when the General kills Carmilla, instead of screaming in pain in the conventional manner of cinematic vampires, Carmilla's mouth relaxes into a soft smile as she realises she has finally been cured of her illness and released into death.

THE DEATH OF HAMMER

> 'Seen today, Ingrid Pitt's seductive performance and Roy Ward Baker's inventive direction conspire to make The Vampire Lovers a better film than it perhaps deserves to be. Brazenly exploitative, it set the tone for Hammer's increasingly explicit direction throughout the seventies.' (Hearn and Barnes, 1997: 137)

Nine years after the release of The Vampire Lovers, Hammer would finally go bust. Throughout those years James Carreras tried to take the Hammer horror productions into new and more profitable territories by combining the studio's tried and tested formula with more exploitative qualities. As the first of these, The Vampire Lovers can be read as an interesting point of transition for the film retains much of the studio's established traditions that have been perverted by the relaxations within the censorship system in which the film's 'explicit blend of lesbianism and viscera would have been unthinkable before' (Hearn and Barnes, 1997: 137). Upon its general release in the UK, the film proved to be popular and signalled that both a sequel should be made (Lust for a Vampire, Jimmy Sangster, 1971) and that the combination of the traditional with the exploitative could work. Subsequently, Twins of Evil (John Hough, 1971) (the third and final tale in Hammer's Karnstein Trilogy), The Hands of the Ripper (Peter Sasdy, 1971), Captain Kronos – Vampire Hunter (Brain Clemens, 1974) and The Legend of the Seven Golden Vampires (Roy Ward Baker, 1974) would follow The Vampire Lovers exploitative qualities amidst a glut of further Dracula and Frankenstein films (such as The Horror of Frankenstein [Jimmy Sangster, 1970] and The Scars of Dracula [Roy Ward Baker, 1970]).

Whilst it is clearly evident that Hammer's final films were motivated by financial and exploitation needs, it is easy to ignore the potential critical value these films hold. In his book Hammer Films, John McCarty acknowledges this through a series of astute readings of a number of these last films, stating that Hands of the Ripper is 'one of Hammer's most interesting films' and that Captain Kronos – Vampire Hunter is 'one of Hammer's freshest, most entertaining vampire movies' and puts particular value upon Frankenstein and the Monster from Hell:

> 'It is interesting to note that as Hammer's series of Frankenstein films progresses, the character of the Baron actually evolves – from a callous, ambitious youth to an effete, manipulative dandy to a murderer and sadist to, finally, a doddering, perverse old man who no longer seems to care if his experiments work or not, so hooked has he become on his capacity for cruelty'. (2002: 46–7)

He concludes by stating that 'Peter Cushing's aging Frankenstein, a senile lunatic in charge of the asylum, is the *real* Monster from Hell and, as usual, steals the show' (ibid.).

From such readings it is possible to suggest that Hammer's final films had the potential to define a new, positive direction for the British horror film to take. But for all their gore, sex, violence and integrity they did not. Instead, it would be the new emerging strain of American horror cinema that would have the most effect on the few British horror films made and released during the seventies:

> 'The Vietnam War had begun. Every night on television Americans were watching the atrocities unfold, their soldiers coming home either mentally scarred or inside a body bag. Suddenly the cuss-free, sex-free, gore-free world of [American] film just didn't ring true. Who would pay to see a cartoonish bogeyman on the screen with the horrors of napalm, massacres and madness played on the daily news?' (Odell and Le Blanc, 2007: 95–6)

With such a political and social backdrop, a group of young film-makers – George A. Romero, Wes Craven and Tobe Hooper – initiated a new wave of American horror cinema: stark, brutal, graphic and explicitly political, their films were a blatant response to their cultural situation. In their films Americans turned upon Americans, brutally raping, murdering and then eating each other. This was a country not only war with itself but one that was, quite literally, devouring itself through extreme violence. But, for all their powerful political commentary, it was not this conceptual value that made these films popular, it was their unflinching approach to gore. In Romero's *Night of the Living Dead* (1968) zombies are seen to eat the recently charred remains of the film's young protagonists whilst Craven's *The Last House on the Left* (1972) contains graphic scenes of rape and torture. As if to go just one step further, Hooper combined both of these qualities within *The Texas Chain Saw Massacre* (1974), resulting in a near 25-year ban in UK cinemas.

Although it would seem that the Great British horror film had died along with its most vaulted patron, this was not the case: whilst Hammer remained firmly entrenched in attempting to rejuvenate their old stories with the new blood of exploitation, a wave of young directors (most notably Pete Walker, Robin Hardy, Piers Haggard, Michael Reeves and Norman J. Warren) were emerging and passing through the genre, bringing with them new ideas, new concepts and more importantly a contemporary approach to British horror. In some respects, these films can be read as a direct response to the crisis in which Hammer had found themselves in: instead of positioning their films within period locales that were haunted by predictable Gothic horrors, these films instead followed the direction American horror cinema had taken by using contemporary protagonists, locations and narratives as their source. As a result, British horror seemed to simultaneously look back at the archetypal template set by *Quatermass* and towards a future of socially aware contexts.

ENDNOTES

[1] Carmilla's death is more brutal in Le Fanu's original text:

'The body, therefore, in accordance with the ancient practice, was raised, and a sharp stake driven through the heart of the vampire, who uttered a piercing shriek at the moment, in all respects such as might escape from a living person in the last agony. Then the head was struck off, and a torrent of blood flowed from the severed neck. The body and head were next placed on a pile of wood, and reduced to ashes, which were thrown upon the river and borne away, and that territory has never since been plagued by the visits of a vampire.' (Le Fanu, 1995: 269)

REFERENCES

Goldberg, Ruth. 100 *European Horror Films* (ed. Stephen Jay Schneider), London: British Film Institute, 2007.

Hearn, Marcus and Barnes, Alan. *The Hammer Story*, London: Titan Books, 1997.

Odell, Colin and Le Blanc, Michelle. *Vampire Films*, Hertfordshire: Pocket Essentials, 2000.

Odell, Colin and Le Blanc, Michelle. *Horror Films*, Hertfordshire: Kamera Books, 2007.

Paul, William. *Laughing Screaming*, New York: Columbia University Press, 1994.

Pirie, David. *Vampire Cinema*, London: Hamlyn, 1977.

Punter, David and Byron, Glennis. *The Gothic*, London: Blackwell, 2003.

Rigby, Jonathan. *English Gothic*, Surrey: Reynolds & Hearn, 2002.

Scheib, Richard. 'The Hunger', Moira (http://www.moria.co.nz/horror/hunger.htm)[Accessed 20/02/08].

Sheridan Le Fanu, Joseph. *In a Glass Darkly*, London: Wordsworth Editions, 1995.

Wood, Robin. 'Burying the Undead: The use and obsolescence of Count Dracula' pp.364-78 in *The Dread of Difference* (ed. Barry Keith Grant), Texas: University of Texas Press, 1996.

The Vampire Lovers (1970). Directed by Roy Ward Baker [DVD], Europe: Optimum Home Entertainment.

Zimmerman, Bonnie. 'Daughters of darkness: The lesbian vampire on film' pp. 379-87 in *The Dread of Difference* (ed. Barry Keith Grant), Texas: University of Texas Press, 1996.

CHAPTER 2: *THE WICKER MAN*

GENRE

The Wicker Man (Robin Hardy, 1973) begins by deceiving its audience: the opening image is a title card which reads: 'The Producers would like to thank Lord Summerisle and the people of his island off the West Coast of Scotland for this privileged insight into their religious beliefs and for their generous co-operation in the making of this film.' This text suggests a declaration of the truth and implies that the film that is to follow is either going to have a documentary quality to it or, at the very least, be based upon real events. Of course, by the film's end the audience realises that it, like the film's protagonist, has been misled all along and that the title card was just the first of these many deceptions. This is not surprising given that the scriptwriter is Anthony Shaffer, 'a notorious lover of puzzles and games [who] has fashioned the screenplay as a conundrum' (Bartholomew, 1977). And so this title card becomes a trick on which Shaffer himself commented:

> 'I think [producer] Peter Snell first thought of it, to lend some outward "reality" to this implausible tale. It's a bit glib – I had two minds about using it – but the intention was to say to people who perhaps were not putting too much attention on the film, "look, this really happened". And it did the trick' (ibid.).

Of all the deceptions within the film, the biggest is the game *The Wicker Man* plays with genre. Because of this, the most significant problem with either viewing or analysing the film is trying to understand *which* genre it operates within. The beginning of the theatrical release of the film suggests horror: a lone member of authority, Police Sergeant Neil Howie (Edward Woodward), flies to the remote island of Summerisle to investigate a report of a missing child, Rowan Morrison. Upon landing, his first interaction with the locals is predictably strained, with the Harbour Master being difficult, resulting in Howie exerting his authority. Once on the island, Howie begins a preliminary investigation but is again met with islanders who are indifferent to both his purpose and his authority. As the night draws in, Howie enters The Green Man pub, looking for 'a room and a bite of

supper'[1]. As he enters the patrons stop singing and talking and an uneasy silence descends as Howie walks towards the bar (Fig. 1). After another difficult conversation, this time with the barman, the patrons return to their drink, conversation and singing.

Fig. 1: Howie amongst the islanders

The difficult locals coupled with the silenced bar is a clichéd moment from numerous horror films (and which is parodied in John Landis's *An American Werewolf in London*, see Chapter 4) and firmly sets out the oppositions of the plot: the outsider arrives in a small, isolated location with a goal that is hindered by the locals' lack of co-operation. It is a convention that some horror films utilise yet at the same time this opening also recalls similar openings to films firmly within the police procedural or, even, the Western genre. In the former, the policeman arrives at the scene of a suspected crime and begins his investigations, meeting resistance from the locals which suggests some sort of foul play or group responsibility for the crime; while within the Western, the lawman arrives at a township on the very edge of the frontier and enters the saloon in an effort to establish both lodgings and the whereabouts of certain peoples. Upon entering, the piano falls silent, the gamblers lower their cards and the drunks lower their glasses.

This generic hybridity – horror, police procedural, Western (and even musical, given the performance of folk songs within the film) – is a shrewd strategy on behalf of its writer Anthony Schaffer and director Robin Hardy, one maintained throughout the film to such an extent that subversion of expectation (of genre, of story and of scenes and sequences) finally becomes the expectation of the audience. But this itself is finally subverted when the film's real ending occurs: having finally solved the crime and rescued Rowan (so it was a police procedural after all), Howie believes he is escaping the island but is instead being led to the real reason for his presence on the island in the first place. By virtue of being both a stranger and a virgin, Howie is to be a human sacrifice to appease the Harvest Gods. Stripped of his clothes and forced into a pyre in the shape of a man, Howie is burnt alive.

This bleak ending finally confirms the film as horror, for the moment is rife with genre traits – humiliation, torture, sacrifice and the very horror of being burnt alive for a heathen God. Yet this scene (like many others in the film), so heavily weighted with the history of the genre, nonetheless successfully subverts convention: instead of sacrificing Howie at night, the islander's faith dictates that he is offered at midday. Setting this scene within broad daylight accentuates the horror. If *The Wicker Man* is, finally, a horror film then the ending is its only scene of true graphic horror. Prior to this scene there has been no other imagery that is associated with the genre (monstrous creatures, vampires, lethal injuries or even a drop of blood). This is ironic because the instigating event of the film's narrative drive is a presumed murder – the ultimate violent act.

Schaffer and Hardy play upon this absence of visual terror tropes by subverting further clichéd scenes from horror cinema. Of all these the most obvious is Howie's ride to Lord Summerisle's baronial home: taken there in a horse and cart, Howie admires the carefully maintained grounds and the flowers in blossom. It is like an Eden yet Howie fails to notice that the topiary has been sculpted into phallic shapes. As Howie rides up the main drive, he turns and witnesses a group of young girls, naked and involved in some sort of ritual. Howie averts his eyes only to look upon the looming architectural edifice that is Summerisle's home. This scene is a parody of Jonathan Harker's horse and cart journey to Dracula's forbidding castle; instead of a demon horse and sinister driver, here is a shire horse and a well dressed driver. Instead of driving through a dark and deadly forest, Howie is taken through a beautiful garden on a summer's day. Instead of there being a dilapidated castle illuminated by streaks of lighting there is a well maintained home set against the backdrop of a clear blue sky. The only concessions to the genre Schaffer and Hardy make are the naked girls (surrogates for the female vampires who seduce Harker) and Lord Summerisle himself – who better to play this role than Christopher Lee, whose career is synonymous with the role of Count Dracula.

THE STARS

Part of the genre confusion lies with the film's two stars – Christopher Lee[2] and Edward Woodward. Prior to their appearances in *The Wicker Man*, both actors were well known to a potential audience: Lee was – and remains – known primarily for his portrayal of Dracula in the Hammer films (*Dracula* [Terence Fisher, 1958], *Dracula, Prince of Darkness* [Terence Fisher, 1965] and *Taste the Blood of Dracula* [Peter Sasdy, 1969]). This role generated a cult following and led to Lee's employment within further horror films. Because of this, it is reasonable to state that Lee is an acknowledged icon not just of horror cinema but also of British cinema generally. Whenever a 'vampiric' villain is required, it is usually Lee who plays this role – Saurman in *The Lord of the Rings: The Fellowship of the Ring* (Peter Jackson, 2001) and Count Dooku in *Star Wars Episode 2: The Attack of the Clones* (George Lucas, 2002) are two of the most recent manifestations of this casting. Lee's sustained profile as a cinematic figure of evil could merely suggest

Fig. 2:
Christopher Lee
as Summerisle

typecasting but, at the same time, his continued activity, 50 years after his first appearance as Dracula, also brings with it a sense of heritage and cultural collateral. It is for this reason that Lee's casting within *The Wicker Man* is both predictable and at odds with the narrative.

The audience expects Lee to be the villain of the film but for the majority of *The Wicker Man*, Lee appears as a warm and gentle man, one who is in sympathy with nature as much as he is in sympathy with the needs of his loyal subjects. He is shown to be calm and intelligent, aware and considerate. He sings and dances, he even dresses up as a woman for the May Day celebrations. All of this defies our expectation of a typical Lee character. It is only at the end, when Howie's fate is revealed, does the audience realise they have, once again, been tricked by Shaffer and Hardy. In the final moments, Lee's performance shifts from that of an understanding laird into a vampire figure of sorts through his 'possession' of the islanders and his manic, bloodthirsty glee at Howie's sacrifice.

A similar inversion of expectation occurs with Woodward. Prior to appearing in *The Wicker Man*, Woodward was well known to British audiences through his appearance in the television serial, *Callan* (1967–72). Woodward played the title character, David Callan, a hard and aggressive secret agent: 'in this role Woodward demonstrated his ability to express controlled rage which occasionally explodes' (Thomas, 2008). With this in the audience's mind, having Woodward play a straight and firm police sergeant would imply that his character would not only solve the mystery of the missing girl but

Fig. 3: Edward
Woodward
as Howie,
the 'Christian
Copper'

would also justly and swiftly punish the perpetrators. So it comes as even more of a shock that by the film's end Woodward's character has not only been duped about the crime but is revealed to be weak and ineffectual, characteristics which lead to his unpredictable death.

NARRATIVE

For all its genre hybridity, the narrative rarely fluctuates from its central context, the conflict between two different religions: Howie's devout Christianity and Summerisle's Pagan beliefs. As the story unfolds, this opposition embodies a range of opposites: the repressed versus the liberated; the controlled verses the uncontrolled; present versus the past; the holy and the unholy; closed mind versus open minds. Although Shaffer's screenplay is balanced, the focus, it seems, is always upon Howie and how his actions / reactions reveal further insights into the island's alternative life style.

A further oppositional conflict exists within Howie himself. In the Director's Cut (2003), the opening scenes revolve around Howie talking to one of his constables, prior to his journey to Summerisle. As they walk along the harbour they pass a wall upon which the graffiti 'Jesus saves' is sprayed (Fig. 4). Benjamin Franks comments upon this brief scene, interpreting it as a further instance of Howie's repression:

Fig. 4: Howie condones the religious graffiti

> 'Howie owes allegiance to the charismatic leadership of Christ, but is able to repress it – at least partially – in the performance of his policing function. Even when he comes across transgression with which he agrees [the graffiti], Howie orders that the message be "removed". Despite his strong beliefs, Howie conducts himself in accordance with the office of the State.' (2005: 69)

THE LEGITIMATE DEPICTION OF SEX

Unlike *The Vampire Lovers* where instances of nudity and sexual relations serve as titillation for the audience, the nudity and sex depicted in *The Wicker Man* are integral to the plot, characters and their actions. Without actually seeing theses instances and acts, the central conflict between the liberal minded islanders and Howie's religion and law abiding morals would not function coherently for the audience.

Whilst waiting for his 'bite of supper' in The Green Man, Howie witnesses the first expression of the islanders' liberal attitudes: when Willow (Britt Ekland), the landlord's daughter, appears for the first time, the patrons of the pub sing a raucous song, 'The Landlord's Daughter', that is rife with sexual innuendo – 'And when her name is mentioned / The parts of every gentleman do stand up / At attention' and 'Oh nothing can delight so / As does the part that lies between her left toe / And her right toe'. Whilst singing, various patrons physically act out some of the actions and make lewd gestures at both Willow (who finds it an amusing complement) and at Howie (who predictably finds the song offensive). As the song reaches its crescendo, Howie stops them by banging on the bar so that he may speak to them about his reasons for being there: 'I think you all ought to know I am here on official business.' This is the first of many instances where Howie attempts to impose his authority upon the island and, by doing so, suppresses the islanders' sense of expression, religious beliefs and their way of living. Here his character begins to polarise for the audience: he is a policeman but his attitudes and reactions begin to suggest that perhaps Howie isn't necessarily the character the audience should be sympathising with after all.

Having eaten his supper, a mildly perturbed Howie leaves the inn and walks over to the village green. Instead of it being a calm space to quietly walk through, Howie is confronted with various couples engaged in sexual intercourse. As the couples writhe about, one woman looks directly at Howie, forcing him to walk away. Through editing, it is suggested that the prolonged image of the various couples making love is from Howie's point of view, particularly given that the shot is a sustained pan across the village green. The duration of the image could easily be dismissed as titillation but it can also be read in two other ways: first, it is Howie's point of view and the length of image either suggests Howie's shock at the public exposure of the couples or a mild erotic response, something that is suggested through the abrupt cut that concludes the shot. The second reading would be that the length of the shot ensures that the audience recognises that all the couples are engaged in the same sexual position – the woman on top of the man. This position immediately suggests female dominance, which is intrinsic to Pagan beliefs, and pre-echoes the next instance of public nudity that Howie encounters.

Turning away from the copulating couples, Howie walks down the road. Hearing a lady sobbing, he looks over a stone wall and sees a naked woman sitting on a grave (Fig. 5). As she cries, she moves gently back and forth. Howie turns and walks away. It is only a brief moment but in relation to the previous image this crying woman connects the act of making love with the act of mourning because the women are all in the same position. This connection between sex and death is a relatively standard one within the horror genre and is usually read as a negative one; but here, on Summerisle, the relationship is positively conceptualised by their Pagan perspective: sex and death are inherently linked

Fig. 5: Sex and death come together on Summerisle

to re-birth, transformation and progression. This connection is reiterated when Howie visits what he assumes to be Rowan Morrison's grave – her umbilical cord has been attached to the tree that grows out of her grave and so unites images of birth, growth and death into one ritualistic space.

Later that night, Howie is woken by a noise from outside. Looking out of his window, he sees Lord Summerisle for the first time. He stands in a white shirt and kilt, his arm around a teenage boy. As he speaks, Howie realises that Summerisle is speaking to Willow and is offering the teenage boy to her for his ritual deflowering. Willow agrees and the boy is sent up to her. As Howie retires back to his bed, Summerisle remains and 'addresses a few lines of modified Walt Whitman to a pair of copulating snails. Speaking of the superiority of animals over man, he observes that "Not one of them is respectable – or unhappy – all over the earth"' (Rigby, 2002: 241).

Of all the scenes that involve the nudity, the most explicit is intrinsic to the film's dénouement: Howie is awoken by the sound of Willow singing. He pauses in his bed, listening to her and then, quietly gets out of bed. Intercut into this action are images of

Willow: naked, she moves around her room, slapping her hands on the bedroom walls and her thighs, running her hands over her body and around phallic objects within the room. As she stands against the shared wall, pressing herself against it, Hardy cuts to Howie in the same position – standing in his bland pyjamas, he too presses himself against the wall and symbolically against Willow's naked flesh (Fig. 6 and 7, below).

This short sequence is intended as a test of Howie's faith. He cannot deny Willow's beauty and so her song and dance functions as a lure in an attempt to seduce Howie into losing his virginity to her. As the scene unfolds, Howie is clearly struggling with the impulses of his 'animal' instinct against his overwhelmingly strong religious beliefs. In the end Howie overcomes his 'primitive' urges and returns to his bed. Within the sequence of events, Howie's refusal of Willow can be interpreted as his first success over the islanders. He remains *intact* and his faith stronger than ever but, as the film ends, it becomes apparent that this was the wrong decision. Had Howie given in and slept with Willow he would have lost his virginity and, as a consequence, would no longer be a suitable sacrifice, implying the islanders would have allowed him to live. But so strong is Howie's conviction that his repression has not allowed him to act in his best interests. It is worth noting that this scene also functions as another instance of Shaffer inverting horror tropes – for the most part, women are punished in horror films for their promiscuity, but within *The Wicker Man* it is celebrated and the man, the one who cannot submit to carnal urges, is punished for his restraint and repression.

Coupling these scenes of sexual freedom with the Pagan rituals seen throughout the film it is possible to suggest that *The Wicker Man* can be read as a reaction to the previous decade: the Sixties became synonymous with individual freedom and led to new and original approaches to art, cinema, music and fashion. It also impacted upon youth culture through aspects of the Hippie movement, the experimentation with drugs and alternative lifestyles as well as an open exploration of sexuality. This shift inevitably began to widen the gap between the establishment and youth culture, where one, by definition, preferred maintaining the status quo, the other wanted greater self expression. Franks opens his text concerning the *The Wicker Man, Demotic Possession*, by stating that 'Director, Robin Hardy, and co-writer Anthony Shaffer, devised the film *The Wicker Man* as a critique of the New Age and Pagan cults that had become a noticeable part of the counterculture landscape of the late 1960s and early 70s' (2005: 63). In this respect, Howie and Lord

Summerisle become signifiers of the times, where Howie stands as the figure of repressed authority and Summerisle as the emerging power of the then contemporary youth culture.

THE FOOL AND HIS THREE COSTUMES

Given that the story's central theme is religious conflict, *The Wicker Man* is, unsurprisingly, replete with a range of symbols. Some are obvious and correlate directly to the Pagan beliefs of the Islanders – the blatantly phallic topiaries within the grounds of the Summerisle Estate are matched by the colourful Maypole within the school grounds, whilst Rowan Morrison herself is, through her suspected sacrifice, a symbolic offering to the Gods – whilst others are more complex symbols relating solely to Sergeant Howie and the fate that awaits him. These symbols can be divided into two groups: Symbolic Costumes and Symbolic Events.

Throughout the film Howie is seen to be wearing three symbolic costumes. The first is his police officer's uniform. This costume is invested with symbolic power, authority and implies the strict control and governance of the law. Yet for its symbolic power on the mainland, Howie's uniform means nothing on Summerisle for the only law they seem to acknowledge is the word of their laird, Lord Summerisle. Acknowledging this, Howie tries throughout the film to re-establish the authority he represents. From the moment of his arrival on the island, Howie calls attention to the power of his uniform: when he calls over to the Harbour Master to send over a boat, Howie says 'as you can see, I'm a police officer' and holds up his arm so that the islander can see the sergeant stripes upon his uniform. Later, when Howie realises he has no control at all, he again points out his stripes but again to no effect. This denial of his symbolic power quite literally reduces Howie's uniform to nothing more than a costume, one that he takes off and replaces with another more symbolically charged costume when he attempts to save Rowan.

The second costume Howie wears is that of the Fool: believing that all the islanders are involved in a conspiracy which will allow them to sacrifice Rowan, Howie takes immediate and somewhat violent action. Taking up a forked candle stick, Howie knocks the landlord, Alder Macgregor (Lindsay Kemp), unconscious. Howie then removes his uniform and replaces it with Macgregor's May Day Costume – a Punch outfit. While Howie understands that this costume will allow him to participate within the celebrations

unnoticed, he fails to understand (or even acknowledge) the symbolic value the costume is invested with: dressed as Punch, Howie is now literally 'playing the fool', the idiot who is unwittingly dancing to his death (Fig. 8). As Miss Rose (Diane Cilento) says: 'You are the fool, Mr. Howie. Punch. One of

Fig. 8: Howie as
The Fool

the great fool-victims of history, for you have accepted the role of King for a day and who but a fool would do that?'

Having being trapped by the islanders, Howie as Punch stands on the edge of the cliffs considering his fate. Despite Howie's protests, Lord Summerisle explains the trap they had laid for him and how perfectly he played the part of the Fool and that it is time to meet his fate. Oak (Ian Campbell), a well built islander, takes hold of Howie and strips him of the remaining Punch garments, replacing it with a simple white smock. This third and final costume gives symbolic form to what Howie actually is in both a literal and symbolic sense – a virgin sacrifice.

Given the overtly religious themes of the film, it is possible to interpret Howie's final costume as a means to render him as a Christ figure: like Christ, Howie is being sacrificed, but not for the sins of the islanders but in an attempt to please the Old Gods.

These readings suggest that the three costumes Howie is seen wearing all represent different facets of what Howie actually is – a police offer stripped of his authority, a fool who does not realise what is happening to him and, finally, the virgin who is ripe for sacrifice. Whilst wearing these symbolic vestments, certain events occur to Howie, which were he less sure of his own convictions and more sensitive to his surroundings, would give him enough clues to his predicament.

The most blatant of these is during Howie's questioning of the school girls: Howie stands at the front of the class behind the teacher's desk, so placing himself in the position of authority within the small classroom. As he questions them, a group of boys are practising a Maypole dance outside the classroom. Howie quickly determines that the girls and their teacher are attempting to deceive him. As he accuses the girls of lying (and threatening the teacher with his authority '…and if I hear one more lie out of you I will charge you with obstruction') he notices that one of the desks stands empty. He goes up to it and opens the lid: a nail has been driven into the bottom of the desk which has a small black beetle attached to it via a length of black string (Fig. 9). As Howie looks down the beetle moves in a perpetually circular motion, the cotton wrapping tightly around the nail and so drawing the insect ever closer to the centre of the nail. The child sitting next to this desk looks at Howie and smiles: 'Poor little beetle. Goes around and around always the same way, you see, until he ends up right tight to the nail. Poor old thing.' Howie looks at her in disgust before asking Miss Rose for the register. Once again Howie, in his mode of righteous authority, is blind to the symbolic value of what lies within the school desk: the nail and the beetle are a physical representation of what is happening to Howie, moving inextricably towards his appointment with the wicker man.

Fig. 9: The beetle going round and round

A further reading of this scene relates the ever decreasing, circular movement of the beetle to the circular dance the boys are making around the Maypole. The nail becomes the Maypole (and so a phallic symbol) whilst the beetle represents the boys (naïve masculinity) who are being steadily drawn into adulthood through the ritualistic movements. This reading equates Howie with the boys, which, to a certain extent, is viable for, regardless of Howie being an adult, his naivety and virginal innocence are all qualities the boys exhibit.

THE SYMBOLIC LANDSCAPE

Instead of the traditional dark and gloomy forest or remote and desolate countryside of Hammer's films, Shaffer and Hardy subvert convention further by setting their film on a picturesque, albeit remote, island. Read purely as a landscape, Summerisle, as its name implies, is depicted as the perfect idyllic rural retreat. With its small, close-knit community, local shops and public house alongside its quaint harbour, the island is an idealised and romantic vision of somewhere to escape to.

Throughout the film the landscape is picturesque and passive with the fields being a vibrant green whilst the gardens and village green are a pale mix of soft blossom and the first flowers of summer. It is all well tended and respected, a quality typified by the grounds of Lord Summerisle's home: with its neatly cut lawns, carefully cultivated roses, and precise gravel paths and drives, the estate appears as if it were a polished tourist attraction. But, standing amongst this quaint and quiet manor, there are small moments of incongruous revelation: the phallic topiaries and the stone circles at the centre of the grounds.

Fig. 10: Howie forms a cross in the Pagan graveyard

Prior to meeting Lord Summerisle, Howie is directed to Rowan's grave by the school teacher, Miss Rose. There, he is told, he will find the body of Rowan Morrison. Before entering into the space, Howie respectful takes off his officer's hat and places it firmly within the crook of his arm. To his dismay, Howie finds the church in a state of ruin and the graves left uncared for. As he walks through the overgrown grass he pauses to read an inscription on one of the tombstones: *Here lies Beech Buchanan – protected by the ejaculation of serpents.* Turning, he is confronted by a woman sitting on one of the other tombstones. In one arm she cradles her breastfeeding baby; the other is outstretched with a single egg resting in the curve of her palm. Howie nods at her and mutters an embarrassed 'Good morning' before walking past her and up to a crypt. Collapsing through neglect, someone has used the crypt as a storage space for punnets and gardening equipment. In a sudden burst of anger Howie knocks these objects to the ground. He then breaks a piece of wood into two and forms a simple cross with it (Fig. 10). As his anger settles he places this Christian symbol onto the cracked lid of the crypt. As Miss Rose told Howie, as a veiled warning before he left for the church grounds: 'The building attached to the grounds in which the body lies is no longer used for Christian worship so whether it is still a churchyard is debatable.'

Yet the church and its antiquated graves form an integral part of both the rural community and the idealised, romantic notions of the countryside. The expectation is that it should be a small stone structure, with heavy wooden doors and eroded gargoyles, surrounded by headstones whose names have long since vanished. What Howie finds is beyond this not just through neglect but through the very perversion of the space itself. To Howie this neglect, the inscriptions and the use of graves within peculiar fertility rites must seem a blasphemy, hence his outburst at the crypt. But, as is becoming Howie's way, he fails to acknowledge that the neglect isn't a rejection of the religious context of the space but the absorption of it: instead of rejecting it entirely, the islanders have absorbed the space, its contents and its religious significance into their own religious beliefs. Here graves are not to be mourned over but to be used to engender new lives and the bodies not left to rot but to remain in state for they are protected by the procreative symbol of the snake.

This idea of absorption is clearly demonstrated in the moments before Howie leaves the churchyard: just as he turns to leave he sees what appears to be a grounds keeper. He approaches this man, saying 'I see you plant trees on most of the graves here'. 'Aye, that's right' replies the man. Howie pauses and then points at one of the graves, the tree that grows out of the burial mound looks young and weak. 'What tree is that?' 'That's a rowan.' 'And who lies there?' 'Rowan Morrison', replies the grounds keeper. They approach the grave and Howie notices an object has been attached to the small branches of the tree. 'What on earth's that? It looks like a piece of skin.' The grounds keeper smiles and tells Howie: 'The poor lassie's navel string, of course. Where else should it be but hung on her own little tree?'

The symbolic nature of the absorption is almost comedic and blatantly directed at Howie's growing insecurities – a rowan tree planted into the grave of Rowan Morrison is as amusingly obvious as it is symbolic. The attachment of her umbilical cord is a more potent symbol and reinforces the idea that death is not an end but a re-birth. Because of these connotations, the umbilical cord also suggests that Rowan is now attached, both physically and spiritually, to Mother Earth and so transforms Rowan's grave from a site of interment into a womb-like space. As a consequence, the churchyard has been transformed from a site of death to one of fertility and re-birth.

On a more complex level, it is possible to interpret the island as a construction that represents an inverted microcosm of established societal concepts. On Summerisle the traditional constructs of law and order have been rejected in favour of personal freedom and an explicitly strong sense of community whilst religion has regressed back to the pre-Christian era of Pagan worship. Because of this the landscape is irreversibly changed: public spaces become the site of private activities, the Christian church abandoned and the graves planted with symbolically charged trees. The agricultural spaces of fields and orchards are also symbolically transformed into the fertile lands of the Gods to such an extent that the whole island can be considered to be a land of the Old Gods.

The only time the landscape becomes threatening is at the film's end: believing he has escaped from the islanders with Rowan, Howie is confronted by Lord Summerisle, Willow and Miss Rose at the cliff's edge. As Howie realises he has been set up, he walks slowly towards the edge and looks over. Large waves crash against the hard, jagged rocks – suddenly out of the passive landscape there is a realisation that Nature can be a violent, uncontrollable and sublime force. One way of reading this scene would be to place it within the context of Nature as God and Howie's impending sacrifice. These contexts subtly suggest that Lord Summerisle is right and the Gods are indeed angry, their rage manifested within the violence of the sea, the turn of its tide and its constant crashing against the very foundations of the island. Angry Gods must be appeased and so they are with Howie, the Christian who will be anointed as a King.

THE DEATH OF THE FOOL

Howie's death is one of the most shocking in all of British cinema: once Howie's plight has been revealed, the expectation is that Howie will either somehow escape or his fellow officers will come to his rescue. Yet, as is typical of this film, the expected does not happen. Instead, Howie is stripped of his clothes and subjected to a ritual that will prepare him for his sacrifice. Realising that he cannot escape, Howie attempts to undermine the Pagan power of Summerisle. He tells the islanders that the failure of their crops is due not to angry Gods but the island's very infertility and that his sacrifice / murder will do nothing to change this concrete fact. Howie then points at Lord Summerisle: '…don't you understand that if your crops fail this year that next year you will need to have another blood sacrifice. And next year no one less than the King of Summerisle himself will do. With the crop's failure, Summerisle, your people will kill you on May Day.' Howie's comment does sting, for Summerisle pauses but then responds: 'They will not fail. The sacrifice of the willing, king, virgin fool will be accepted.' But it is enough. The seed has been sown, a seed of Summerisle's possible downfall planted in the minds of the believers.

Upon seeing the wicker man[3] (Fig. 11), Howie screams 'Oh God! Oh Jesus Christ. Oh my God! Christ!'. This line of dialogue is ambiguous. As Christopher Lee comments in his DVD commentary, this is a Christian cry for help yet it could also be interpreted as a blasphemy – another of the film's oppositions. Howie's words ultimately resist firm interpretation and perhaps that is the significance of this single line of dialogue, that when faced with the horror of his sacrifice, Howie may be confronted with a different understanding of his faith: he may be asking for a deliverance or intervention that will not come. But, as he burns within the wicker man, Howie does experience deliverance, of sorts: Lee states during the DVD commentary that in the burning heart of the wicker man, Howie accepts his sacrifice for it will bring him closer to Christ, as both were sacrificed for the need of others. Such an interpretation is implied and consolidated when the islanders' deception is finally revealed to him: before placing him in the wicker man, the women of the island strip Howie and, after the brief ritual, dress him in a white

gown. In this plain symbolic dress, Howie is equated with Christ, lifted above the crowd, his arms outstretched, crucified upon the complicity of the islanders and carried to Oak, one of the strongest of the islanders. Lowered to the ground, his hands are then bound before he is dragged to his cross, the wicker man.

Fig. 11: 'Oh God! Oh Jesus Christ!'

ENDNOTES

[1] Shaffer's constant stressing of difference between Howie and the islanders is even worked into the scene where Howie eats his supper. Pushing the food around his plate, Howie comments to Willow '…it's just that most of the food I've had – the farmhouse soup, the potatoes, the broad beans – have all come out of a can.' Howie, as the modern man, eats 'fresh' food from a can where as Willow and the other islanders literally eat fresh food that they have grown and harvested themselves.

[2] It is worth noting that Shaffer wrote the part of Lord Summerisle explicitly for Christopher Lee and that Lee was so taken with the script that he worked on the film for free (Rigby, 2002: 239 – 40).

[3] Edward Woodward did not see the wicker man until that point in order that his reaction be as genuine as possible.

REFERENCES

Bartholomew, David. 'The Wicker Man' in *Cinefantastique*, Vol. 6, No. 3, Winter 1977.

(http://www.wicker-man.com/articles/cinefantastique_TWM_article_1977.pdf) [Accessed 24/01/08].

Franks, Benjamin. 'Demotic Possession: The Hierarchic and Anarchic in *The Wicker Man*' pp. 63-78 in Murray, J., Stevenson, L., Harper, S. and Franks, B. (eds) *Constructing The Wicker Man*, Glasgow: University of Glasgow, Crichton Publications.

Rigby, Jonathan. *English Gothic: A Century of Horror Cinema*, Surrey: Reynolds & Hearn, 2002.

Thomas, Ann-Marie. 'Edward Woodward'

(http://www.screenonline.org.uk/people/id/457985/index.html) [Accessed 25/01/08].

The Wicker Man: The Director's Cut (1973). Directed by Robin Hardy [DVD], Europe: Studio Canal.

CHAPTER 3: *DEATH LINE*

Gary Sherman's *Death Line* (1972) begins in a seedy manner: a blur of neon colours steadily pulls into focus to reveal the silhouette of a man in a bowler hat standing in front of a porn theatre in London's Soho. He pauses, taking in the sights on offer and then turns and walks out of shot. Instead of cutting, the camera pulls back out of focus and dissolves from one blurred image to the next, following this person as he tours the area. The garish neon lights, the pockets of darkness and camera repeatedly pulling focus on the images of topless women in the theatre foyers present Soho as a seedy quarter, a quality reinforced by the accompanying soundtrack – a suitably sleazy rendition of 'The Stripper'. As the sequence comes to an end, the identity of this person is revealed to the audience: a well groomed middle-aged man in a black suit, tightly trimmed moustache with a black umbrella hooked over his arm. He steps out of a strip joint, putting on his black leather gloves before venturing out into the cold streets. This man, later to be identified as Sir James Manfred OBE (James Cossins), appears to be the archetypal 'dirty old man', the sexually repressed British bachelor visiting the darker and seedier sights of London (Fig. 1-4, overleaf).

Fig. 1-4: Seedy London

Throughout this simple montage a number of *Death Line*'s thematic concerns are made evident: in terms of representation, the sequence suggests a gritty (and grimy) sense of realism will be deployed during the film whilst the image of a clean, respectable businessman in the heart of this seedy space blatantly suggests a sharp contrast between social classes[1] as much as between people and places. With the camera consistently lingering upon the black and white photographs of naked women, the sequence subtly suggests that flesh, naked or otherwise, is both a commodity and something to be drooled over. On a more complex level, the use of blurs, pulling focus and dissolves, suggests a different kind of film-making in that the standard way of presenting the story has been rejected in favour of a more creative, expressionistic approach to narrative depiction. These qualities steadily pervade the unfolding narrative, rendering *Death Line* as a remarkably bleak and 'oppressive film which deserves credit not least for a realistically shocking take on urban alienation in an industry still floundering in gothic melodrama' (Marriott and Newman, 2006: 124).

The sequence concludes with Manfred walking down to Russell Street Tube Station. As he walks down to the platform, the audience hears the first dialogue of the film, a muffled shout of 'Mind the doors!' before the revving hum of a tube train leaving the station. As Manfred walks down the platform, he sees a woman who he approaches and, when close enough, stops her and whispers into her ear. The woman looks shocked and says 'You filthy…' but Manfred interrupts her. 'You little flirt. How much?' he says in a crisp upper class voice as he opens his wallet. 'Piss off' responds the woman but when she sees the handful of notes Manfred is holding she pauses then reaches out for the money. Manfred smiles, pulling away the money, 'Payment on delivery my darling', he smirks. She smiles at him then, abruptly, kicks him in the groin, taking the money from him as he doubles up. The woman runs away, whilst Manfred staggers over to the seating. As he does so the position of the camera changes, shifting from the unseen observer to that of an unknown character as the camera lurches towards Manfred. Given the way in which the camera moves and the manner in which Manfred reacts, it is obvious that whoever this person is, they are clearly a threat.

PATRICIA AND ALEX

The last tube pulls into Russell Street Station and a young couple step off and onto the platform. They are Alex Campbell (David Ladd) and Patricia Wilson (Sharon Gurney), students studying in London and on their way home. As they walk out of the platform them come across a body of a man, slumped face down on the stairwell (Fig. 5). Their reaction to this discovery demonstrates another instance of contrast: Alex continues to walk past the body whereas Patricia stops and asks Alex to help him. Alex responds by saying 'Leave him alone, he's a drunk'. From this brief line of dialogue Alex is identified as American, and his response suggests an uncaring nature. Instead of leaving the man Patricia kneels down by his side and tries to turn him over. Alex complains, but Patricia is concerned, suggesting 'He might be a diabetic. See if there is a card in his wallet.' Alex sighs and gives in to Patricia's request. Finding his wallet, Alex reads out the man's name from one of his club cards, 'Sir James Manfred OBE' and cynically comments: 'No diabetic, Trisha. Just a drunk, a titled one.' Further contrasts become evident here – Alex is unsympathetic to the prone man whereas Patricia demonstrates a more caring and concerned attitude towards others. There is also the contrast between Alex being an American and Patricia being British, made all the more apparent when Alex reacts to Patricia's concerns by saying 'Trisha, in New York we walk over these guys' to which Patricia responds, 'We are not in New York.' Their brief argument ends with Alex stating that he '…doesn't want to get involved'. Alex's comments also suggest a negative attitude towards to the homeless. This indifference to the plight of others will reverberate later into the film, particularly when the circumstances of the film's antagonist are fully

revealed. The scene concludes with Alex and Patricia going to get help from a police officer. But, when they return to the tube station, Manfred's body has gone. What was initially assumed to be just another drunk has now become a missing person and, against his wishes, Alex is now inextricably involved in this man's disappearance.

Fig. 5: Pat, Alex and Manfred

INSPECTOR CALHOUN

In contrast to *The Wicker Man*'s Sergeant Howie, Inspector Calhoun (Donald Pleasance) is far from that of a repressed, by-the-book police officer. Instead he is shown to be both aggressive and casually corrupt, a seemingly cynical and heartless character who is slowly coming to the end of his tether (Fig. 6). He is, in some ways, that clichéd world-weary policeman, steadily worn down by criminals and by the bureaucratic system within which he has to operate. His anger and frustrations are demonstrated through aggressive humour and any chance to disrespect those in authority: when his Detective Sergeant, Rogers (Norman Rossington), tells him about the report of Manfred's body going missing, he responds by saying 'James Manfred, that rings a bell. He's some big shit… err… shot at the Ministry of Defence or the Home Office' and later mocks Manfred further by saying 'O B bloody E'. His aggression extends to all those he encounters, including Alex: having had him bought to the station for questioning, Calhoun begins the questioning in a civil

Fig. 6: Calhoun, the British Copper with his tea

manner[2] but soon turns on Alex by accusing him of stealing from Manfred. When Alex responds in an equally aggressive tone, Calhoun mocks him further by saying he should go back to school where there might be a protest march for him to join. Alex gets up and walks out of the office, just as Calhoun shouts out after him 'and get your hair cut!'

Whereas Howie stuck to the law virtually to the letter, Calhoun is more than happy to bend it. When he and Rogers later search Manfred's study, Calhoun tries to open the drawers but they are locked. 'Suspicious bastard' says Calhoun as he takes out his lock pick. As he attempts to break the lock, Rogers looks on disapprovingly, not that Calhoun is bothered by this. Once the drawers are open, he rifles through the paperwork and helps himself to a handful of nuts from a bowl on the side table. He then helps himself to a glass of whiskey. He offers a glass to Rogers who declines, saying 'not while I'm on duty, sir'. Calhoun drinks a mouthful and retorts 'pompous ponce'.

It is ambiguous as to whether the audience is meant to identify with Calhoun or not. As an officer of the law he is corrupt at a superficial level yet his concern and need to resolve the issue of Manfred's missing body demonstrate a dogged willingness to achieve. In some respects he wants to solve the case as a matter of professional pride, but there is, perhaps, another motive: that he is entertained by the idea of a working class police inspector lording it over the upper classes in the line of duty.

THE LAIR

The camera steadily pans from right to left as it slowly moves through the horrendous lair of the film's antagonist: shifting out of a murky darkness, the camera moves along the ruptured surface of a crudely carved tunnel. As it moves the sound of the water dripping fades out as the camera glides across a severed arm. The elbow joint is a mass of mutilated flesh, whilst parts of the arm and fingers appear to have been chewed open and the bones gnawed upon. Rats scurry around the rotting limb, squeaking as they nibble at the flesh. Beneath the half-eaten fingers is a pool of maggots, writhing in the dirt. The camera continues to move from right to left, entering into another area of darkness. The sound of dripping water has returned and is overlaid with the sound of a heart beat. As this steady pulse reverberates in the background, the camera enters into a patch of light in which Manfred sits. He is not dead, but close to it. He sits slumped against a rock, his face pale, and his eyes staring blankly into the darkness. The camera passes him by and takes in more bodies. Their chests are gouged open, eyes are missing, and their faces are flayed of flesh. The sound of the heart beat steadily stops and, in turn, is replaced by the sounds of simpering. These are human sounds, the sound of someone injured. Moving through the half-darkness the camera then passes over what appear to be supplies – canisters of oil, candles and mining lamps – before finally entering into a crude living space.

Still moving from right to left, the camera continues through this space in which a woman, pregnant and in distress, lies on a makeshift bed. Beside her crouches a long-haired man. He tries to comfort her as the camera passes them by. From here it seems to pass through the crudely carved wall and out into the dark, brick-vaulted tunnels of the underground. Lit with a pale yellow light, the camera continues to track through this space of repeated arches. As it does so the events of a tunnel collapse are played through non-diegetically: the sound of picks striking the hard stone and of spades turning the earth coupled with muffled voices. There is a quiet rumble and the picks stop falling; a pause, then the sound of the roof collapsing; screams amongst the sound of the rubble settling and then silence.

The *mise-en-scène* of this single track shot, lasting just under three minutes, suggests that this part of the underground is an organic space, for its rough surfaces are slick with dripping water and congealed blood. The dirt is mixed with rotting bodies forming a ground of putrid flesh whilst the walls are adorned with chunks of flesh, decaying bodies and bones. With the sound of the slowing heartbeat overlaid, this hidden part of the underground becomes not a living, breathing space but a dying space, one that is littered with decay and putrescence.

In addition, the continuous tracking suggests that the space depicted is historically 'trapped': as the camera pulls back through the vaulted tunnels, a historic event is played out through a montage of sound. Like ghosts, the sounds are an echo of the past literally reverberating into the present as the camera passes through the walls and out into the present day tube station. This reading is compounded by the camera's movement itself as it pulls forward from a location bound to the past into a location that is physically bound to the present.

The tracking shot concludes with the camera seemingly passing through the solid wall of the underground and out into the bright and reasonably clean[2] platform of Russell Street Station. Waiting amongst the other passengers is Patricia. After a few moments a train pulls in and she gets on with the other passengers, leaving the platform empty.

THE LONDON UNDERGROUND

The London Underground has a long association with the British horror film. The origins of this relationship began, once again, with Professor Bernard Quatermass where, in *Quatermass and the Pit* (originally broadcast on the BBC in 1958–9 and then later remade by Hammer [Roy Ward Baker, 1967]), he is called in to investigate a series of archaeological discoveries made during extension work on the Central Line, near Hobbs End station. As Quatermass examines the site and its ancient artefacts, a further discovery is made as what appears to be a space vessel is unearthed. Whilst some consider it to be a Nazi propaganda weapon, Quatermass believes it to indeed be a crashed spaceship. The narrative culminates in the manifestation of an alien 'Satan' over the London skyline as Quatermass realises, with some horror, that the human race is the product of alien intervention. With the space ship looking like an unexploded bomb and the ghostly appearance of the Devil, the conclusion of *Quatermass and the Pit* is an explicit representation of nuclear imagery and anxiety as the 'bomb' 'explodes' and releases a terrifying mushroom cloud over London as its citizens flee in panic.

From such an apocalyptic beginning, the London Underground would be visualised as a space that was rife with symbolic potential. So often used by film-makers, the location has itself become a recurrent motif within contemporary British horror cinema: *Death Line* is most obvious whilst John Landis would later use Tottenham Court Road station as one of the hunting grounds for *An American Werewolf in London* (1981). More recent descents into the Underground have been explicitly grounded in the space, as with Christopher Smith's *Creep* (2004) and with the matricidal climax of *28 Weeks Later* (2007).

Within *Quatermass*, the Underground was positioned as a site of a buried past and one that has alarming repercussions within the present day upon its discovery. In this respect, the alien space ship is no different to the Gothic trope of the past returning to haunt the present, bringing with it a terrifying revelation of our ancestry whilst simultaneously acting as a precursor image to our possible destruction. Such qualities make parallels with *Death Line* for both narratives deal with a long buried secret, its consequence upon the present and with its perverse sense of evolution. But whereas *Quatermass* suggested the latent horrors of the emerging Cold War and of a potential nuclear strike against Britain, *Death Line*'s contextual agenda can be read as something more psychological and more repressed. These readings are both embodied within and amplified by the Underground: the warren-like tunnels and the echoing chambers all give physical form to our psychological space and therefore function as symbols of the unconscious (Fig. 7 and 8). In this reading of the location, the Man who wanders those lonely corridors becomes a manifestation of our human fears – a repressed anxiety of losing our essential humanity through impoverished circumstance, through neglect and through ignorance.

Fig. 7: The
Underground
as a familiar
space...

Fig. 8: ...and as
an unknown
space

THE MAN AND THE WOMAN

Throughout a number of the films analysed within this book, the monstrous element is perceived not as something evil but more tragic: Carroon, the astronaut in *The Quatermass Xperiment* becomes infected and transforms into a monstrous creature against his will, as does David Kessler in *An American Werewolf in London*. There is Victor Frankenstein's creation, a man made of corpses who is abandoned by his father and there is Carmilla, a lonely vampire who seeks only an eternal love. Although monsters, these characters are also victims, largely because of the vicissitudes of fate – Carroon, David and Carmilla do not want to kill but by virtue of their unnatural states have to, and Frankenstein's Creation merely wants to understand and be accepted for who he is and not *what* he is. Amongst these characters is the antagonist of *Death Line*: simply described as The Man (Hugh Armstrong) within the credits, this representation of the narrative threat is perhaps the least deserving of all subjects to be termed 'monstrous'.

The audience first see the Man during the aforementioned tracking shot. Seen from behind, he crouches down by what is assumed to be his partner, who, like the Man, is merely described in the credits as The Woman (June Turner). During these moments, the audience does not see much of this Man's face and body. Instead, what little glimpses of him that are seen are feminised – he has long black matted hair, his fingers are thin and pale and the vocal sounds he makes are no different to those made by his partner. Whilst the Man holds her hand, he tries to comfort her by stroking her hair and pulling a blanket over her in an effort to keep her warm (Fig. 9). His efforts, it seems, do alleviate the woman's suffering so the Man leaves her for a moment and wanders into the recesses of their living space, returning with the body of James Manfred. He hauls the body onto the bed and, lifting up Manfred's head, he slices open the man's throat. Blood pours from the wound and into the Woman's mouth. Although his physical appearance and these actions are monstrous, the intentions of the Man suggest he may not be a monster *per se* – tending to the sick Woman implies he has feelings for what the audience assume is his family: that he understands she is in pain and wants to help in whatever way he can.

As the blood continues to froth at the wound, Sherman cuts to a tight close-up of Manfred's face and from there steadily pan's upward and over the face of the Man: whereas James Manfred's face is smooth and clean, with neatly trimmed moustache and tightly cropped hair, the Man's face is ruptured with bloody, weeping sores. His skin is pale and tight, his beard as greasy and as matted as his long hair, his teeth black and broken. The contrast is obvious and almost unnecessary – where Manfred is the clean, urbane and modern male of upper class society, the Man is the dirty representation of the past, a member of the working classes left to struggle for survival. It is a moment in which the poor are quite literally eating the rich.

Sherman cuts again from the dark, unpleasant space of the liar to another bright, clean space – the opulent home of James Manfred. Calhoun and Rogers let themselves in and admire the room: an ornate fireplace dominates the room, whilst each wall is decorated with an original oil painting. On the mahogany desk stands a jewelled clock and gilt letter opener. The room is a grand space, an expression of comfort and an arrogant display of wealth. Sherman has cut from the impoverished and filthy home of the Man to Manfred's home of excess. The contrast is again obvious, but as Calhoun and Rogers search the room, more comparative than contrastive elements start to emerge to the extent that Manfred's study is in fact another type of liar. Calhoun notices something amiss with the bookcase and, using a lock pick he works away at the join between the shelves and manages to spring a lock. The bookcase opens up and reveals a small red room, containing only a chair, table and television monitor. On the screen is a coarse black and white image of Manfred's bedroom, indicating that a secret camera has been installed in there. The perverse nature of this room, coupled with the red and black colour scheme, suggests a parallel with the Man's lair. Both are seedy places, both are drenched in the limited palette of red and black and both are spaces in which secrets are hidden, unifying the rich with the poor.

THE MAN AND PATRICIA

Having spent the night at the theatre, Alex and Patricia take the tube home. Pulling into Russell Street Station they alight but Patricia realises she has left her books on the tube. Alex quickly gets back onto the tube, picks them up but doesn't make it to the doors in time. They both laugh and Patricia says she will see Alex when he gets home. As the tube pulls away, Patricia is left alone on the platform and, suddenly, the Man appears and kidnaps her.

Given that the Man is the monstrous antagonist, the audience assume that he is, probably, going to either kill Patricia and eat her or abuse her, possibly both. But this does not happen. Instead, the Man takes her down into his lair and puts her onto the makeshift bed. He places a blanket over to keep her warm whilst she lies unconscious. When she comes around, she begins to scream as the room is swarming with rats. The Man comes into the room and starts to kill the rodents, battering them with a spade, stamping on them and, finally, picking one and biting off its head. It would appear that the Man doesn't intend harming Patricia. Instead, he wants to protect her and seems to treat her as a replacement for the deceased Woman.

Unable to comprehend this, Patricia thinks the worse and manages to affect an escape by battering the side of the Man's head. Whist he staggers around in pain, she runs out of the lair and into the vaulted underground tunnels, eventually hiding in a dark corner in an effort to elude the now pursuing Man: with an oil lamp to illuminate his way, he walks slowly through the darkness, calling out the only words he knows, 'Mind the doors'.

This single line of dialogue places great emphasis on the tragic nature of the Man. Although his intentions for Patricia are dubious – he wants her company and presumably to procreate with her – he is also only acting on impulse and instinct. He has no intention of actually hurting her, with his actions instead suggesting that he wants her more for companionship than anything else. As he searches the tunnels he repeats the dialogue over and over again, calling out to her with the only words he is capable of communicating with. When he finds her he does not attack her. Instead, he crouches down and, holding out his hand, he gently enquires 'Mind the doors?'. Although Patricia screams and tries to push him away, he continues, repeatedly saying 'Mind the doors'; with each repetition the emotional inflection changes, again eliciting sympathy for the Man. With his diseased and ruptured skin, his emotional empathy and his pursuit for companionship, the figure of the Man is comparable to the Creation in Shelley's *Frankenstein* (1818): both are made of sick flesh, both are capable of emotional expression and both long for an equal.

Upon returning to their flat, Alex finds it empty and soon realises that Patricia may have been abducted by the same person who took Manfred and so begins his own exploration of the Russell Street underground. Armed with a torch, he walks through the tunnels and comes across the rubble from the collapsed roof. Amongst the debris is Manfred's bowler hat. Cutting between Alex and the Man, Sherman steadily builds the tension, even more so as the vocal inflections of 'Mind the doors' turn from gentleness to anger. Losing his patience with Patricia (or perhaps merely venting his frustration that he cannot properly communicate with her), the Man attacks her and upon hearing her screams, Alex appears and manages to pull the Man away. They fight and eventually Alex bests the Man by repeatedly stamping on his head.

Alex's assault on the Man is quite graphic, but as much in its relationship to the exchanges at the start of the film than to the violence. Alex's first lines of dialogue indicate he is an uncaring person and that his opinion of the homeless is less than charitable. These qualities imply that Alex's vicious attack can be interpreted as if it were a physical expression of his disgust at such people. Instead of using sufficient force to restrain or frighten the Man away, Alex repeatedly stamps on his head. As he does so, Patricia keeps screaming at him to 'leave him', her concern for the Man's beating overriding her fear of him. The violence is made all the more acute because, ultimately, the audience's sympathy lies not with Alex, the presumed hero of the film, but with the Man, the misunderstood antagonist.

ENDNOTES

[1] Sir James Manfred OBE is clearly of the upper class, shown here to be in Soho where he is paying to watch working class woman strip for his pleasure.

[2] Moving from the dark and filthy space of the underground to the clean and bright space of the tube station creates another significant moment of contrast within the film. Also, because of the historical nature of the Man's liar, there is a further contrast between his past and Patricia's present.

REFERENCES

Death Line (1972). Directed by Gary Sherman [DVD], Europe: Network / Granada Ventures Ltd.

Marriott, J. and Newman, K. (eds) *Horror: The Definitive Guide to the Cinema of Fear,* London: André Deutsch Limited, 2006.

CHAPTER 4: AN AMERICAN WEREWOLF IN LONDON

'An American Werewolf in London *is not a comedy. It's called a comedy. They keep calling it a comedy – it's very funny I hope – it is not a comedy.*' (John Landis, director of *An American Werewolf in London* [1981], 2002)

As if to make this genre confusion blatantly clear Landis opens his film with a montage of images of the Yorkshire Moors: it is presented as a wilderness space, empty, barren and desolate, a cold wind pushing against the leafless trees. There is no evidence of man-made structures until the final image, a pale grey road, winding its way through the hills and dwarfed by the surrounding countryside. These establishing shots present the film's initial location as a sublime space, as a landscape in which there is beauty but also desolation, an inherent danger or violence. The audience can't see it but they can feel it through the sparse and rugged terrain. These qualities are contrasted, in a typical *auteurist* trait of Landis's, by the soundtrack. Instead of the sound of the hollow wind blowing across the land there is Bobby Vinton's spirited rendition of *Blue Moon*. The joke is two-fold – not only does Vinton's happy voice contrast with the dark and sinister moors, the lyrics describe meeting a loved one in light of the moon. Given that the film's title has already appeared over the landscape montage, the correlation between a werewolf's horrific lunar transformations is contrasted against the joyful union Vinton sings of. In this brief opening sequence, Landis's directorial and genre agenda are set: wherever there is horror there will be comedy, and where there is comedy there will be horror. And, without giving the audience chance to fully absorb this, Landis presents his next joke through the introduction of his protagonists, David Kessler (David Naughton) and Jack Goodman (Griffin Dunne).

A truck drives down the grey road, coming to a stop at a crossroads. The driver, a farmer, gets out of his cab and walks to the back of the truck, taking out the locking pegs on the truck doors. As he lowers the hatch, two young men are revealed to be sitting amongst a flock of sheep (Fig. 1). The farmer helps them out and points them in the right direction, telling them that the village of East Proctor is only a few miles further down the road. As he gets back into his cab, he looks back at them and says 'Boys, keep off the moors. Stick to the roads and the best of luck.' He smiles and pulls himself up into his driving

Fig. 1: David and Jack, lambs to the slaughter

seat. With this warning consolidating the unnamed terror of the moors, the joke becomes even more obvious: those two young men, David and Jack, are quite literally lambs ready for the slaughter. To make sure the audience get this joke, Landis reinforces it by naming the only pub in East Proctor 'The Slaughtered Lamb'.

ORIGINS

While working in Yugoslavia as a runner on *Kelly's Heroes* (Brian G. Hutton, 1970), Landis was driving through the countryside when he was unable to continue his journey because of a Gypsy funeral. Getting out of his car, Landis watched as the gypsies buried the corpse at a crossroads. The body was wrapped in a canvas shroud which has then been wrapped with garlands of garlic and rosaries. The body was then lowered, feet first into the grave. 'He was being buried this way so he doesn't get up and cause mischief… and I kept thinking what if he did get up?' (Landis, 2002).

Although *An American Werewolf* was the first script written by Landis, it would become his fifth film. His debut feature, the low-budget *Schlock* (1973), written, produced, directed and starring Landis as the title character, would set a template for Landis's subsequent directorial career through its sense of comedy (childish, sometimes puerile but more than often visually orientated gags) coupled with a range of cinematic references that were reconfigured though the comedic elements. Although Landis had tried to gain studio backing for *An American Werewolf*, many executives were put off by the combination of horror and comedy, feeling that the audience would struggle with the narrative – should they laugh or should they be scared? The success of *Schlock* enabled Landis to go on and write and direct a series of popular American comedies – *The Kentucky Fried Movie* (1977), *National Lampoon's Animal House* (1978) and *The Blues Brothers* (1980). With each being considerably successful, Landis became a viable director and was allowed to return to his *Werewolf* having now secured the necessary backing.

Considering those early films in respect to *Werewolf, auteurist* traits soon become evident; but, unlike the stylistic or content driven motifs or other auteurs, Landis's authorial stamp is evident in his repeated use of format and reference: the majority of his films feature a comedic duo (and in one case, a trio) of men: first appearing in *The Blues Brothers*, they then appear in *Trading Places* (1983), *Spies Like Us* (1985), *The Three Amigos* (1986) and *Coming to America* (1988). In each film the partnership functions on the essential comedy trope of the straight man paired with the fool. Landis tends to enhance this relationship by making one of the male duos a little more sensitive, a man who is a little more in tune with the world and a little more tolerant of it. With these characteristics in place, the man and his partner fool will encounter a series of obstacles which they resolve by either working together or by sheer luck and faith. The audience's pleasure comes from watching them repeatedly fail, confident in the knowledge that they will achieve their narrative goal by the end[1].

A CONNECTICUT YANKEE

The title, *An American Werewolf in London*, is a playful reference to the 1839 novel *A Connecticut Yankee in King Arthur's Court*. Written by novelist and humorist Mark Twain, the story concerns Hank Morgan, a superintendent at an arms factory who is knocked unconscious when he receives a blow to the head during a 'misunderstanding'. When he comes round, Hank finds himself inexplicably transported back to Camelot in sixth century England. As Hank becomes accustomed to his new surroundings, his character traits begin to emerge, particularly his rationalist approach to life which makes it difficult for him to deal with the historic people and their superstitions. The parallels between Hank's story and David's are evident here: David is effectively the Connecticut Yankee in contemporary Britain whose rationalist approach to the supernatural is the beginning of his undoing. Instead of listening to both Jack and the locals at The Slaughtered Lamb, David repeated fails to acknowledge the possibility of the supernatural. Even after the werewolf attack, his confrontation with the rotting corpse of his friend and his eventual transformation, David still searches for a rational explanation ('I must be going mad!'). It is only when confronted with the corpses of his victims does he finally relent and accept that there is 'something' other than the real and tangible within the world. In this respect the narrative of *An American Werewolf* becomes a cruel and viscous Rite of Passage for David: he is first punished for not believing in the possibility of the supernatural (attacked by the werewolf) and then punished again (becomes cursed and must die) when he fails to accept such possibilities even in the very face of them.

DAVID AND JACK

Together, David and Jack form Landis's comedy duo[2], with Jack playing the fool to David's more serious and emotionally charged straight man. The film begins by establishing this relationship through their dialogue and during the scene within The Slaughtered Lamb: as they enter into the warmth of the pub, all of the patrons go silent. Drinks are put down, the last dart thrown and everyone turns to face them. Being polite, David asks: 'It's very cold outside. May we come in?' There is an uneasy pause then the landlady, a burly Yorkshire woman who leans over the bar, nods her head and the boys smile and begin to take off their rucksacks and coats. As they do so, the patrons turn back to their drink and conversation. The landlady comes over to them and asks what they would like to drink and, after a series of rebuttals, David orders them both a cup of tea. As they talk to the landlady, Jack, in a heavy-handed way, makes a joke about remembering the Alamo, but it is a joke that predominantly only Americans would understand. The landlady looks down at him and replies that she does remember the Alamo: 'I saw it once in London, in Leicester Square.'

As they wait for their tea, Jack nudges David and points to a strange red symbol etched into the wall between two burning candles (Fig. 2). David shrugs when Jack informs him that it is a pentangle. The significance of this is lost on him so Jack continues, telling him that 'Lon Chaney Jnr. at Universal Studios maintained that's the mark of the Wolf Man.'

David still doesn't seem as bothered about it as Jack and, before their conversation can continue, they are interrupted by one of the patrons, a big, bald headed man (played by Brian Glover)[3] who turns his chair around to face them as he shouts out to the pub in a thick Yorkshire accent: "'Ere, Gladys, Tom, did you hear the one about the crashing plane?'

Fig. 2: The mark of the wolfman

The pentangle has a dual narrative function: it is used as both a device to highlight the difference between David and Jack and to imply that this pub is central to the terrors to come. In relation to the protagonists, Jack's response to the symbol is typically childish and correlated to the fictional world of cinema, a world which Jack clearly believes in for he finds the presence of the symbol highly suspicious as much as it arouses his superstition. David, on the other hand, feels it is better just to ignore it. Ironically, however, the audience soon learn that it is Jack's response that has the greater validity.

As Glover's character tells his joke, Jack repeatedly pushes David to ask about the symbol. David refuses and tries to listen to the joke which ends on the punch-line 'Remember the Alamo!' Everyone in the pub bursts out with laughter, including David and Jack but through his laughter, Jack leans over to the man and asks about the pentangle. Everyone stops laughing; the darts player misses the board. No one speaks, and the atmosphere becomes more threatening. Outside there is a roll of thunder and David suggests that they leave. As they gather up their coats and rucksacks, the landlady addresses the pub – 'You can't let them go' – but Glover's character simply replies 'Go and God be with you.' The landlady tries to intervene again but the darts' player turns to the boys and tells them to go: 'Stay on the roads. Keep clear of the moors', to which the other man adds: 'Beware the moon, lads.'

Leaving The Slaughtered Lamb, David and Jack begin their hike towards the next village. As they talk they slowly stray off the road[4] and head out into the moors where their conversation is interrupted by a horrendous howl. Instead of being frightened, the two look at each other and engage in a brief dialogue that reinforces the light-hearted nature of their relationship, with each suggesting to the other possible reasons for the howling – a coyote, the Hound of the Baskervilles or Heathcliffe. As they laugh and joke, Jack realises it is a full moon and another blood curdling howl drifts across the moors.

As they begin to run back towards the safety of the pub, David slips in the mud. Both boys laugh and the anxiety lifts. Jack smiles as he leans down to take hold of David's hand only for a creature to leap onto him and kill him. The creature then attacks David, only for it to be shot dead by the locals. As David slips into unconsciousness, he rolls over to one side and sees the corpse of a naked man, three gunshot wounds in his stomach.

With Jack dead and David transported to London for medical treatment (the precise location of The Slaughtered Lamb and moors is unclear, but the accents are certainly 'northern'), it is assumed that the comedic partnership between them is now over. But, with this being a comedy-horror, such a relationship is essential and so Landis brings Jack back from the dead. Within the mythology of this narrative, those killed by the werewolf remain in a state of limbo until the killer's bloodline is severed. This aberration within death conveniently allows for Jack to visit David and, in doing so, inform him of his obligations.

These appearances are at first quite conventionally unsettling and disquieting, with Jack frightening David by sitting on the end his bed, his face raked open and his throat hanging in bloody tatters. Although he appears in a dreadfully traumatised state, Jack has maintained his sense of humour and attempts to dispel some of the horror through wry jokes: in an effort to try and dispel the horrific state of his torn body, Jack asks David if he can have a piece of his toast. As Jack eats, he tries to explain to David what has happened (including attending his own funeral and stating that its 'boring' talking to corpses) and what will soon happen to David, come the next full moon. David, ever the realist, thinks he is either imagining Jack or slowly loosing his grip on reality, trying to terminate their conversation by saying 'I will not be threatened by a walking meat loaf!'

As the film progresses, Jack's re-appearances become more comic, even as his body decays. By his final scenes he is nothing more than a talking skeleton, his flesh dried tight to his skull, his white teeth glistening. But, even in this state, Jack tries to help David by convincing him that there is no cure for the werewolf's bite and that in order to free both him and all those that he has so far killed, he too must die.

REPRESENTATION: THE RURAL BRITISH

Fig. 3: The insular and suspicious locals

The Slaughtered Lamb sequence presents the rural British as a suspicious and insular group of people, a typical horror film stereotype of any rural persons (Fig. 3). They are unsure of anyone from the outside of their close-knit community, partly because they are not simply from 'around these parts' but more so because of their superstitious knowledge and understanding. When David and Jack leave, the Barmaid tries to stop them but the pub patrons band together and agree a pact that effectively sends David and Jack to their deaths. This pact is not made out of malice towards these two outsiders but more because of what Glover's character says: 'Should the world know our business?' David and Jack effectively become a sacrifice in an effort to keep the outside world at bay.

In the end, moral consciousness works its way into the group on two occasions: first when they attempt to save David and Jack when the werewolf attacks; and, secondly, when David's doctor investigates David's claims personally. These two instances act as a confessional exorcism of the community's guilt and although it does not fully exonerate them of their crime, it does, in cinematic terms at least, suggest that these people are not fundamentally bad people. Instead, they are scared of the werewolf but even more scared of the contemporary world, and its likely reaction to the secret at the heart of their community, should it be revealed.

In many ways this construct – the rural outsiders who are privy to arcane knowledge and experience – is a classic trope of the horror genre. They are feared by the modern for this very knowledge yet, conversely (as with those in *An American Werewolf*) the very same people fear the exposure of this knowledge to the modern. Such feelings emphasise the cultural divide and suggest that such rural people are bound to a mythic past where Nature and their response to it is inextricably dictated by folklore. Such readings suggest comparisons between the villagers of East Proctor and the islanders of *The Wicker Man*'s Summerisle. Both groups of people are bound to the landscape, to their traditions and to their superstitious belief systems but whereas the people of Summerisle have no proof conclusive of their beliefs, the locals of East Proctor do. Here lies their fundamental difference for the islanders fear a debunking of their belief systems by those from the modern world whereas the villagers of East Proctor keep their secret to protect the outside world for the werewolf is a tangible, living manifestation of their beliefs and of their fears.

This mode of representation bleeds into the readings of the landscape: like the fields of Summerisle, the Yorkshire Moors (to repeat, the precise intended location of 'East Proctor' is unclear and the viewer must interpret it from the landscape and the dialect of the locals) are not just a bleak and barren pastoral but a landscape that is inextricably bound to those tales from folklore, ones sustained by the many generations of East Proctor. These myths become evidently real at Jack's expense (as they do to Sergeant Howie on Summerisle) and so transform the bleak pastoral into the dark and violent hunting grounds of the supernatural.

DAVID AND ALEX

A further partnership within the film is the developing relationship between David and his nurse, Alex Price (Jenny Agutter). As she cares for his physical health, Alex falls in love with him and, upon been discharged, takes David to her home to continue his recuperation.

For the role of Alex, Landis chose British actress Jenny Agutter (Fig. 4). Trained as a dancer, Agutter came to prominence through her performances in *The Railway Children* (Lionel Jeffries, 1970) and *Walkabout* (Nicolas Roeg, 1971). In both films Agutter plays a teenage girl on the cusp of maturity and one who must use all of her available

Fig. 4: Jenny Agutter as Alex

resources in order to overcome the increasingly dire situations of the narrative. Part of the credibility and consequential success of her performances lay in the very fact that Agutter was only a teenager herself when she played these roles, with the characters' emergence from childhood into young adulthood reflecting Agutter's own experiences at the time. Brian McFarlane comments upon Agutter's career after these films as an example of 'how difficult it has been for a young and gifted actress to maintain momentum in British cinema. As a result, she has worked frequently in America and on TV, but only infrequently in British films' (n.d.).

Casting her as Nurse Alex Price suggests a number of readings: initially, Agutter is a quintessential English lady – attractive, reserved, with her delicacy matched by her emotional strength and resolve – and so makes her the ideal choice to play Alex for she too is a woman of restraint and strength. Such qualities recall Agutter's key roles for she again plays a character that must use all that she has in order to overcome the trials of the narrative. In this respect, Landis is coyly playing a role reversal for the narrative of *An American Werewolf* can be read in a perversely similar way to *The Railway Children* and *Walkabout* – all three are preoccupied with emergent sexuality and the drama of coming of age.

Agutter's relaxed performance coupled with her clean, crisp English accent add further weight to the national texture of the narrative and provide a further parallel to the populace of East Proctor: there the women are shaped as much by the land as the men are, with the only female seen at the village being the Barmaid. Although she is homely and clearly quite caring, she shares with the men a no-nonsense approach to life. Alex too shares a motherly affection towards David, initially providing somewhere for him to stay only to become his lover. She also listens to him, supports him and tries to protect him. Such is the extent of her affections for him that she risks her life for him and, finally, like the Barmaid from East Proctor, gives in to superstition in an effort to save the man she loves.

LOVING THE WEREWOLF

From the opening scenes of David and Jack walking towards East Proctor, their dialogue indicates that Jack views relationships with the opposite sex as if he were still a sexually frustrated teenager whilst David, more mature and more respectful, perceives love as something you come across by chance and is to be treated with care and with respect. With his emotional position declared, when David begins to seduce Alex, the audience accept this as a viable part of the narrative instead of a mere plot device. Because the audience's sympathy already lies with David, his relationship with Alex seems as if it is simultaneously doomed yet possibly the one way in which David can be freed of his curse. Having made love, David and Alex talk, with David asking her if she ever saw the Universal film *The Wolf Man* (George Waggner, 1941). He continues by saying that in that film only true love could save the Wolf Man. Lying in the bed, naked and with the scars from the wolf's attack upon his chest, this line of dialogue comments on both their developing relationship and hints at a possible conclusion: although cursed perhaps David can be saved by Alex, suggesting this film will not end as all other werewolf films do with the death of their protagonist. With these qualities being made evident, the narrative of *An American Werewolf* shifts from comedy / horror to tragic love story. On reading the first draft of the script, David Naughton commented that 'I thought it was a fairly straight forward tragic love story. Tragic in the sense that here are these characters that don't really have any control over what happens to them... he falls in love with a nurse and ultimately succumbs to the tragedy of being a werewolf' (Auden, 2006).

David's conversation with Alex about werewolf films is just one of the many instances of the complex and layered sense of intertextuality within the film: David talks about these films not only as fictional constructs ('...the Universal film...') but as if these films are not based on folklore but on proven fact. In his current state, Hollywood does not offer David horrific entertainment but a possible solution to his curse, even though Jack has consistently impressed upon him that he must die in order to be free. Whilst these intertextual comments suggest a wry humour on Landis's part, they also compound David's sense of confusion and loss as they are presented as a moment in which a young man is trying to come to terms with a life-threatening 'illness'. With such readings, the developing relationship between David and Alex takes on a more emotional (and tragic) depth for it may just be that that can save David from his cursed fate.

Carefully worked into the subsequent scenes that chart the development of David and Alex's relationship are sequences which depict David's understanding of his supernatural condition. The first such instance is a series of dreams: during one of them David is back at his family home, sitting at the dining table completing some revision. His mother is in the kitchen whilst his father reads a newspaper. His younger brother and sister, Max and Rachel, sit watching an episode of *The Muppet Show*. The images are of a stable, middle class domesticity, a calm and safe space in which David has grown up in and can now put the horrific attack behind him. As he looks down at his textbook the door bell rings. His father opens the door and is confronted by three Nazi soldiers, their faces monstrously disfigured. They burst into the house, quickly shooting David's parents. Whilst one sets fire to the curtains, another holds a knife to David's throat and forces him to watch his siblings being murdered (Fig. 5 and 6). As the monster screams, he slices open David's throat. David wakes up in his hospital bed and sees Alex next to him. She tells him in a gentle voice that it was just a nightmare and that she has a good cure for such dreams. She stands and crosses to the room's curtains. Pulling them open she reveals one of the monstrous Nazis who stabs her repeatedly in the chest. As he screams in terror, David wakes up again, this time for real.

Fig. 5 and 6: David's nightmare

Landis has commented that he wanted the dreams to be as 'realistic' as possible. To do this, Landis felt that their content and imagery would only be things that were emotionally pertinent to David: 'In *Werewolf*, [David] is afraid he is losing his mind and so his dreams have to relate to his own experience which is why he thinks of his family where it's safe, and because he's a Jewish-American kid who grew up with images of the Nazis' (Landis, 2002). Given this, it is worth noting the presence of Alex in this and the other dreams, which clearly signifies that she is somebody who is as important to David as his family and so consolidating their developing relationship.

A more complex reading of this dream is offered by William Paul who suggests that 'this blurring of boundaries between conscious and subconscious parallels the blurring boundaries between internal and external' (1994: 400). This reading is more pertinent to another of David's dreams in which he sees himself running, naked, through an area of woodland. He pauses behind a tree, watching a young deer graze. David leaps onto the animal, biting open its neck as he does so. As Paul suggests, this dream clearly unites David's subconscious knowledge and fears with the imminent bodily transformations he will soon undergo. For all his outward and waking denial, his subconscious informs him of the truth and so binds him to the tragic fate of all cinematic werewolves – their only chance of escape or release from their curse lies in their own mortal death.

DAVID TRANSFORMS

The transformation sequence is an essential component of the werewolf film. It is the most anticipated moment as it not only provides the spectacle of transition but is also the most explicit visual signifier. Inherently involved in this scene is the technical quality of the special make-up effects. Such is the extent of this that readings of the subsequent monster hinge upon it. As Paul comments, the early transformations in films such *The Wolf Man* were created through a series of cross dissolves in between which more hair was applied to the actor's face and hands. This rudimentary process meant that the subsequent werewolf 'walks upright like a man and keeps his clothes on like a gentleman. The handling of the transformation makes it easy enough to see the underlying allegory about the beast in man since the beast still appears to be a man' (1994: 384). This idea of man-as-beast was given a grotesquely spectacular rendering 43 years later in Neil Jordan's *The Company of Wolves* (1984). As a symbolically loaded film, the men do not transform into wolves but physically shed their skin to reveal the wolf within themselves. In two of the film's most elegant images, one man peels off his skin to reveal the musculature beneath, which then distends into a wolf's snout, whilst another man's back rips open as the wolf breaks free of the constraints of human skin. Either way, the symbolic value remains the same – man is beast and the beast is man.

From an *autuerist* perspective, a number of Landis's films include a scene in which the lead character briefly looks directly into the camera. Known as breaking the Fourth Wall, this momentary glance disrupts the viewing experience. Instead of the audience passively observing events unfold, they are acknowledged by the character through a glance, a stare or even a knowing wink. This awareness suggests collusion between spectacle and spectator, a moment in which the fabricated reality of the film pauses and reality is allowed to invade. During David's transformation this occurs twice, once to further engage the audience's sympathy for the character and the second time to frighten them.

The transformation begins[5] with David sitting in Alex's living room, reading a book. He suddenly screams out and, dropping the book, takes hold of his head. He gets up and screams out again, 'I'm burning up!' and rips of his shirt and takes off his trousers and pants. Standing naked, his body is covered in sweat and in horror David raises his hand which is starting to painfully distend into a paw. He the drops to the floor calling out to Jack for help. His body convulses as it grows thick patches of hair. 'Please help

Fig. 7 and 8: David transforms

me, Jack,' David manages to say; 'I didn't mean to call you a meat loaf.' More hair grows and his spine arches and ripples. Rolling onto his back, David, virtually covered in hair and his teeth extending into fangs, looks directly into the camera and reaches up with his mutating hand, begging for the audience's help. The viewer's horror at the startling transformation merges with their sympathy for David. They are helpless and can do nothing but sit and watch the remainder of this terrifying spectacle unfold (Fig. 7 and 8).

David now kneels in profile, sweat running down his face. His jaw distends, forcing his face forward and out into a wolf snout. He screams again as his neck follows similar mutation before cutting to a close-up of his closed eyes. They are covered in sweat and when they open they look directly into the audience, two glassy green eyes, and the pupils vertical slits of black. David, the American werewolf in London, howls.

SEX AND THE WEREWOLF

One of the overriding relationships between various werewolf films is the strong connection between sex and the anticipated transformation scene. Whereas *The Company of Wolves* deals with this seemingly inherent genre trope through symbolism, *The Howling* (Joe Dante, 1981) embraces it fully and uses it as one of its set-pieces: two of the film's characters make love deep within a forest. As they reach their orgasm, both begin their transformations, literally becoming werewolves as they get closer to their climax. The explicit union of sex and transformation reconfigures the idea of Man as Beast. Here, the Beast is not something supernatural, but manifestations of Man's most primitive urge – to reproduce – and so the werewolf's metaphoric value is consolidated as a visual signifier of the primitive and the animalistic.

Within *An American Werewolf* it is of no coincidence that David's first full on-screen transformation takes place only hours after he and Alex have first made love. This narrative order of events is coupled with the manner in which David's transformation takes place: as previously described, David first gets hot then he strips himself naked before his body and limbs, in a blatant set of phallic representations, begin to enlarge and elongate. Because of the juxtaposition with the sex scene, David's transformation can be interpreted either as the moment he comes of age or as a symbolical manifestation of his masculinity. In the former interpretation, David's bodily changes accompanied by the simultaneous growth of hair replicate the bodily changes that take place during puberty. In the latter interpretation, puberty is perceived as the moment when one emerges into adulthood and so David's transformation therefore becomes a shedding of his childhood 'skin' as he grows into his adult skin. With either reading, puberty is visualised as something that is horrific, a transformation that we must all endure as our bodies change without warning or consent. As Landis comments:

> 'Essentially, it's an erection metaphor. A lot of it has to do with adolescence. The whole thing of metamorphosis, when your body is changing, that's what puberty is about. You're getting hairy; all of a sudden your dick's getting hard. These weird things start happening to you.' (2002)

DAVID GOES ON THE RAMPAGE

David's story began on the cold, wind-swept Yorkshire moors. There, the barren landscape was a forbidding, isolating place and its inhabitants equally sinister: in the warmth of The Slaughtered Lamb sit the locals, all male and a mixture of ages but all dressed in working clothes that suggest they work on the surrounding farms. The man who tells the joke typifies them all with his strange looks and his thick no-nonsense Yorkshire accent. In contrast to these working class locals, the people David encounters in London are quiet, restrained and seemingly middle to upper class. The majority speak in clear English accents and would appear to be employed within the city. London itself is depicted as a vibrant and cosmopolitan space, a modern space of bright lights and the tube trains full of punks, a contrast to the clichéd cinematic representation of London – red buses, telephone boxes[6], and Bobbies on the beat.

Of all the scenes set in London, the most spectacular takes place within the Underground. Whereas Gary Sherman imbued the London Underground with horrific potential in *Death Line* through set dressing and lighting, Landis generates fear by *removing* the majority of the same location's essential qualities: the large volumes of people moving through the space, the sound of buskers and platform announcements, the clatter of footsteps and the sharp whistle of passing trains are all subtracted to leave a cold, empty warren of tiled corridors. In this state the location becomes a subtle contradiction for it is still recognisable (and so contributes to the national texture of the film) but it is also one that is alien due to these absences (Fig. 9).

This transformation of the ordinary is an essential quality of any contemporary horror film. The trend for the haunted baronial castles and fog shrouded graveyards that once dominated the Hammer films has long gone and has instead been replaced with locations that are easily and readily identifiable by the contemporary audience. By allowing an audience to recognise a space as opposed to a set of generic tropes, the horror of the narrative becomes more real and, as a consequence, heightened. With films such as *The Wicker Man*, *Death Line* and *An American Werewolf*, it would seem then that horror is no longer grounded safely in the past but firmly and frighteningly evident within the present. This shift in location and timeframe has also meant a shift in the nature of monster. They are not supernatural beings anymore but are something 'other': beings that reflect the essence of Carroon, the contaminated astronaut from *The Quatermass Xperiment*;

Fig. 9: The American Werewolf attacks Gerald Bingsley

for these creatures, like the cursed David Kessler, now have a very human core and haunt very human spaces.

DAVID DIES

The final act of *An American Werewolf in London* continues the relationship between horror and comedy, sex and transformation whilst sustaining the tragic nature of David's situation: finally accepting that his friend Jack is right, David goes to a telephone box to call his parents. Much to his dismay, the phone is answered by his younger sister. During their conversation David tries to express his love for all his family while his sister, clearly bored, ignores these final declarations. David concludes by saying 'Please don't forget what I told you about Mom and Dad… that I love them. And I love Max and I love you too… I do, no, I'm not being silly you little creep. You promise, OK? You be a good girl then… Yeah, I love you. Goodbye.' David puts down the phone, takes out a penknife and attempts to kill himself. Unable to do so, he puts the knife away and steps out of the phone booth to see a very decayed Jack standing in the entrance to an adult cinema.

As David pays his entrance fee, Landis positions the camera so that David occupies the left-hand side of the frame whilst the right-hand side is filled with lurid pornographic images. One of the posters declares the title *See you next Wednesday* with the tag-line *a non-stop orgy!*. In his analysis of *An American Werewolf*, Paul comments that '…in the context of the film, the phrase carries a double meaning since we see it toward the end of the most extended violent sequence in the film, a non-stop orgy of killing' (1994: 383). It is subtle, but Paul's interpretation is valid, for the subsequent scenes are indeed a non-stop orgy of sex and violence, gore and death.

During the entire adult cinema sequence, Landis rapidly shifts the tone from humour to horror then back again, unsettling the audience's expectations of what is to occur next. This disruption of expectation is fluid and coherent within the context of the narrative so it never disrupts the viewing experience. Instead, it actually works to build more tension and anxiety in the viewer. By constantly changing the rules and by infusing the horror with humour (and vice versa) the audience simultaneously feels afraid (what horror is to come next?) and safe (it's OK, we can laugh at this).

The adult cinema sequence draws to an end with each of David's victims offering him options of how to kill himself. This dialogue is filled with intentional humour as the corpses discuss the pros and cons of various suicide methods yet, at its heart, this isn't funny for David, the character with whom the audience's sympathies lie, for he is going to have to die. Perhaps the audience has already acknowledged that this can be the only ending for David and so the anticipation of his impending demise is all the more tense and all the more tragic. The sequence concludes with David transforming for a second time and, again, the transformation is coupled with sexual imagery: as David grips the chair in front of him, his body thrusts back and forth; his motions mirror the sexual thrusting that is taking place on the cinema screen. As David groans in agony, the couple in the film moan in sexual ecstasy – pleasure and pain together again.

Having transformed, David breaks out of the cinema and into Piccadilly Circus. His first violent act is to leap onto a police officer. Not content with just biting out his throat, David bites off his head. Another police officer stares in horror as his colleague's head bounces across the bonnet of a patrol car and out into the road. What happens next is typical of Landis[7]: the werewolf runs around Piccadilly Circus, snapping at pedestrians' feet and ramming into cars, causing a series of grotesque set-pieces within a massive pile up: a red double-decker bus swerves to avoid the monster only to crash into oncoming cars; bodies are thrown out of the window screens and, landing in the road, run over. People are pushed to the floor or through shop windows. Others are crushed between crashing cars. Although only lasting a few moments, the Piccadilly Circus sequence is manifest of Paul's comment that the ending is indeed an 'orgy of non-stop' violence (1994: 383).

The violence continues as 'David' runs through the streets. The armed police finally corner him in a dark and dirty alleyway. As the police aim their rifles, Alex pushes through, finally managing to break through the cordon and into the alley where she carefully approaches David: crouched and ready to pounce, the creature looks up at her as she says 'David, please let me help you... I love you, David.' There is a pause and the werewolf's lips settle back over its teeth and its eyes widen. Perhaps the 1941 Universal film was right, love

Fig. 10: David finally released from the curse

can kill the beast and not the man but, in this harsh realistically depicted tale of contemporary werewolves such myths are void and the werewolf lunges forward. The police open fire and kill the beast. In the end there are no silver bullets, no love lifting this terrible curse: just David, naked and pierced with bullets, lying dead in the gutter (Fig. 10).

ENDNOTES

[1] A further, more amusing, *autuerist* trait of Landis is evident in the repeated use of the phrase 'See you next Wednesday' in Landis's films. This was taken by Landis from a sequence in Stanley Kubrick's *2001: A Space Odyssey* (1968) in which astronaut Frank Poole watches a video of his parents. As they wave goodbye to the camera and wish Frank well, they say 'See you next Wednesday'. The phrase appears in various contexts throughout Landis's oeuvre, usually in a humorous or incongruous context.

[2] Studio executives had hoped that Landis would cast Dan Ackroyd and John Belushi as David and Jack respectively, due to the actors working so successfully together on Landis's previous film, *The Blues Brothers*.

[3] Brian Glover is a well-known British character actor famed for his Yorkshire accent. Glover grew up in Barnsley, Yorkshire and supplemented his student grant by wrestling (under the name of Leon Aris the Man from Paris). Having graduated, Glover taught English and French alongside another teacher, Barry Hines. Hines would go on to write *Kes* (Ken Loach, 1969) and suggested that Glover take the part as the games teacher within the film. From there his acting career began and developed into writing. Glover once said of acting 'You play to your strengths in this game. My strength is a bald-headed, rough looking Yorkshireman.' His gravestone reads *Brian Glover 1934 – 1997 Wrestler Actor Writer.*

[4] It is worth noting that David is wearing a hooded red jacket. This coupled with his wandering off the safety of the path makes a subtle correlation to another wolf narrative, *Little Red Riding Hood*.

[5] Prior to David's transformation, he wanders aimlessly around Alex's flat, looking for something to do. He tries reading a book but soon gets bored so he switches on the television set. In his book *Nightmare Movies*, Kim Newman comments that 'An American Werewolf is the first horror film since *Death Line* to puncture British feelings of superiority over our transatlantic cousins. When David tries to find something worth watching on the much-vaunted "best television service in the world" he gets a choice between a darts' match, the test card and an advert for the *News of the World*' (1988: 180).

[6] As a sign of the times, the red phone box in which David makes his final call to his parents has graffiti relating to the seminal UK punk band *The Sex Pistols* all over it.

[7] This multiple car pile up is reminiscent of the similar multiple car pile up that ended *The Blues Brothers*, indicating a further directorial trait – Landis's love of vehicular destruction.

REFERENCES

An American Werewolf in London (21st Anniversary Edition) (1981). Directed by John Landis [DVD], Los Angeles: Universal Studios.

Auden, Sandy. 'Getting naked: *An American Werewolf in London* revealed: An interview with David Naughton', 2006 (SFSite.com, http://www.sfsite.com/10a/dn233.htm) [Accessed 05/03/08].

Landis, John. 'Interview with John Landis' in *An American Werewolf in London* (21st Anniversary Edition) [DVD], Los Angeles: Universal Studios, 2002.

McFarlan, Brian. 'Jenny Agutter' in *Screenonline* (http://www.screenonline.org.uk/people/id/564158) [Accessed 29/05/08].

Newman, Kim. *Nightmare Movies: A Critical History of the Horror Movie from 1968*, London: Bloomsbury, 1988.

Paul, William. *Laughing, Screaming: Modern Hollywood Horror and Comedy*. New York: Columbia University Press, 1994.

CHAPTER 5: *HELLRAISER*

CLIVE BARKER AND CONTEMPORARY GOTHIC

As a writer, artist and film-maker, Clive Barker's work is unified by a series of *autuerist* traits: regardless of the medium, his imagery has a preoccupation with the monster, the transformation of the human body and the exposure of the open wound. These repeated elements are usually contextualised through characters that are marginalised, engage within transgressive sexual activity or through the notion of the aberrant family. From these characteristic elements emerges Barker's aesthetic and metaphoric approach to horror – injuries to the body become beautiful and function as violent moments that positively transform the individual. As a consequence, Barker's short stories, novels and films are unique for they invert the genre's negative tropes into positives: the haunted ancestral home, the disfigured monster and the uncanny supernatural event all function as horrific moments of reflection, revelation and powerful instances of self awareness.

Because of this, horror exists on the periphery of the banal existence of daily life within Barker's narratives, with the numbing routines of work and domesticity waiting to be ruptured by the emergence of the monster. And, when these creatures do emerge, they are both terrifying and liberating for contact with such glorious beings forces Barker's protagonists to redefine themselves, to defend (or surrender) their values and beliefs as much as their bodies and their families. With such preoccupations, the majority of Barker's work can be considered to be re-workings of the Faust myth where the pact-maker and the pact[1] are all reconfigured to fit and reflect current society. At their very essence, Barker's work presents this seemingly unholy pact as a potentially positive aspect for the horrific consequences have the power to liberate through the confirming act of confrontation – that is if his characters survive the nightmare of the narrative.

To contextualise these directorial motifs it can be suggested that Barker's work can be interpreted as a contemporary manifestation of the Gothic: established in aspects of literature during the eighteenth century, the Gothic has become a unique genre for its traits and style have been successfully absorbed into other mediums, be that film, music or fashion. This apparent absorption into other forms makes genre definition increasingly difficult yet undeniably allows a universal sense of the Gothic to be formed.

In literary and filmic forms, the generic traits of the Gothic are the haunted ancestral home, the monster, the figure of the vampire, the concept of the liminal body and the occurrence of the Uncanny. Inherently involved within these broad concepts are smaller elements such as the labyrinthine space that leads to an attic or dungeon in which unspeakable acts of torture are committed, the revelation of an alternate world, acts of violent rage and terror, sexual perversion and the implication of incest. As this chapter will discuss, all of these elements are present, in one form or another, within *Hellraiser*, clearly indicating that the film is a manifestation of the contemporary Gothic.

With Barker's novella *The Hellbound Heart* (1986), upon which *Hellraiser* is based, it would seem that Barker took all of these elements and successfully fused them with his own fertile imagination from which he derived a wholly original piece of British cinema: rejecting the theatrical sense of the Gothic that Hammer and its imitators adopted, Barker positions his narrative within the dull grey world of Thatcher's middle England. Here everything is tangible and real, bland and mundane, a repressed set of class archetypes waiting to be threatened by the intrusion of the intrinsically unreal monster or vampire. Herein lies *Hellraiser*'s greatest achievement – instead of populating the narrative with a clichéd Gothic monster, Barker makes his human characters the monsters, pushing their bodies and morals to immensely violent and destructive boundaries in order to create his manifestation of evil. To compound this, Barker contrasts these human monsters with a quartet of supremely Gothic creations – the Cenobites – and so creates a narrative where the idea of the monstrous is in a constant state of flux.

THE CENOBITES

The four Cenobites function as the most blatant manifestation of the Gothic / cinematic monster within *Hellraiser*: these mutated individuals seldom appear but, when they do, their appearance is a brutal shock because of the bodily tortures they have each endured. The terror these creatures induce can be considered as an aesthetic shock as opposed to an emotional terror, for their bodily corruption represents a fastidious order within the extreme chaos of pain: the cranium of the lead Cenobite (Doug Bradley) is carefully inscribed with a near perfect grid, a nail driven into the flesh at each intersection. His body is evenly flayed and carefully dissected. Each hook and pin is aligned with the leather garments stitched into his skin, each mirrored on the opposite side. His three companions are as equally abused, their exposed flesh glistening in the crisp blue light that only occurs in their presence. Their leather smocks shine, the barbs of the fish hooks that pierce their skin glint, as do those that hold the flaps of peeled flesh taunt. Each extreme act of tearing, ripping, peeling and pinning has been carried out with a delicate precision, their appearance crafted not by torturers but by some perverse and dedicated artist. Such is the power of their image that they represent in narrative terms 'a whole culture' (Howe,

1987) in that far greater horrors are implied by their appearance and their dialogue: 'We have such sights to show you' intones the lead Cenobite to a terrified Kirsty (Ashley Laurence), sights which are briefly glimpsed in the dark, labyrinthine corridors of Hell and the grotesque creature, the Engineer, who roams this maze.

Fig. 1: 'Pinhead', the lead Cenobite

The Cenobites' appearance has a two-fold and interrelated function – first it correlates with Barker's interest in the wound and, secondly, generates meanings in relation to the film's Gothic potential: the Cenobites' flayed skin is literally peeling back what Barker has termed 'the veil' and so exposing what lies beneath the skin-thin barrier. The camera briefly lingers upon these traumas and allows the audience to literally look into the wound. For some this moment is horrific, painful and sickening whereas for others this moment may be shocking but it is the wound's very beauty that horrifies. For all their grotesquery, the Cenobites exist as balanced, aesthetic objects – beauty manifesting itself on the very edge of bodily destruction. Here, the monster's outward appearance is in itself a representation of their duality – when Kirsty asks who they are the lead Cenobite cryptically replies 'Angels to some. Demons to others.' By declaring this duality upon their very skin, the Cenobites function as liminal bodies and so, conceptually, ground themselves within the Gothic.

Within her catalogue of defining attributes of the literary Gothic, Kelly Hurley discusses the frequent appearance of opposition, particularly those oppositions that are predominately and meaningfully located within the transformation of the human body: '…bodies that occupy the threshold between the two forms of opposition, like human / beast, male / female or civilised / primitive' (Hurley, 2002: 190). Hurley describes these transforming beings as possessing liminal bodies, bodies which are 'admixed, fluctuating, abominable' (ibid.). When applied to the Cenobites, their claim to be liminal bodies exists in their visual connotations for they are beautiful and disfigured, visually ordered but physically corrupted.

For such potentially significant and symbolic figures, Barker provides the Cenobites with very little screen time and, when they do appear, it is more to talk than to physically act: instead of functioning in a violent and destructive manner like the majority of cinematic monsters, the Cenobites predominately stand still and engage in conversation. This dialogue is a further subversion for they talk in a coherent and fluid manner that uses language as power, as a further mode of impressing their authority upon others. They also speak quite poetically – 'Bearable isn't it? The suffering of strangers, the agony of friends…' Communicating in this manner consolidates their inherent power and forces further control upon their bodies: instead of unleashing their evil in physically violent acts, they repress it and allow it to manifest itself in their language and gestures, in their tone and voice.

FRANK AS MONSTER

'Generally [in horror movies] the monsters don't talk about their condition… What I wanted Frank to be able to do was have dialogue scenes, even romantic scenes that play between him and Julia. I wanted Frank to be able to stand around and talk about his ambitions and desires because I think what the monsters in movies have to say for themselves is every bit as interesting as what human beings have to say. That's why in Stalk and Slash films I feel that half the story is missing. These creatures simply become, in a very boring way, abstractions of evil. Evil is never abstract. It is always concrete, always particular and always vested in individuals. To deny the creatures as individuals the right to speak, to actually state their case, is perverse – because I want to hear the Devil speak. I think that's a British attitude. I like the idea that a point of view can be made by the dark side.' (Barker, in Edwards, 1998)

In some respects it is very easy to interpret Frank (Sean Chapman / Oliver Smith) as a contemporary reborn Frankenstein's monster for he is a man, brought back from the dead by the accidental spilling of his brother's blood. And, just like Frankenstein's creation, Frank is sentient. He can think, communicate, seduce and ultimately manipulate, allowing Barker to simultaneously render Frank human and monstrous in his outward appearance and in his psyche. By making his central monster human, Barker allows for audience identification that generates a certain amount of ambiguity where Frank is concerned and it is this uncertainty that identifies Frank as the archetypal Gothic monster: confined to the attic in his partially resurrected state, he frustratingly patrols the border between reality and the dimensions of Hell, continually marking out the line he crossed in the pursuit of exquisite pleasure. In this respect, Frank can be seen to represent the transgressed for he is the one who has explored the supernatural and has, in one form or another, been able to return to tell his tale. But there is nothing heroic about Frank. He is malevolent and perverse, seeking further self gratification in his desires for flesh, for Julia (Claire Higgins) and, ultimately, in his incestuous desires for Kirsty.

Symbolically Frank hardly represents repression – the coda usually associated with the monstrous Other – but its opposite, complete liberation. His sense of liberation embodies all aspects of his life until his first encounter with the Cenobites who, literally, liberate him of his flesh and blood in their combined pursuit of extreme experience. Because of this Frank can be seen to represent desire or, at the very least, the extremes of desire.

Within this consistent pursuit of sexual experience, Frank's ambiguity is compounded for he is constantly seeking liberation, even though the Cenobites have given him just that through the liberation of his flesh. His open attitude towards sex and sexuality is embodied within all aspects of his representation: he is the first character to appear, seemingly naked and sweating with the camera lingering on his tanned and muscular torso. He is clearly heterosexual, which is confirmed when Julia later finds a photograph of him with a naked woman. Yet, Julia's recollection of him, instigated by this photograph, is curious for her memory of him interprets him as if he 'is straight out of a Kenneth Anger film, all tattoos and gay biker styling' (Le Blanc and Odell, 2001: 88). Beneath his black leather jacket, his tight white t-shirt again emphasises his muscular physique, the rain that falls around him running down his chiselled features. It is almost as if he is constantly naked, an ironic visualisation given that Frank appears for the most part of the film stripped of his flesh. The peculiar combination of representation implies bisexuality, a feeling which pervades most of the film for even though Frank expresses a continued sexual desire for Julia, he also speaks of the painfully pleasurable sexual transgressions with the Cenobites. His sense of sexual liberation reaches its limit when, moments before his death, he hisses to Kirsty, 'Come to daddy.'

But for all of this Frank's only true desire is to regain his flesh and become 'human' again. Yet this physical change would only be superficial for Frank's psychology – as repeatedly demonstrated throughout the narrative – remains as transgressive as it was prior to his bodily destruction: his desire for flesh can only lead to further sexual encounters, further aberrance and further transgressive acts.

FRANK AS VAMPIRE

The origins of the contemporary vampire lie within the folklore traditions of Eastern Europe. Here the vampire is not the decadent sophisticate popularised by Bram Stoker's *Dracula* but a filthy peasant, a wretched creature who preyed upon their own family or neighbours in an effort to slake their thirst for blood. In fictional terms their purpose was to symbolise the spread of disease, to give a physical and human form to plagues. Although the vampire remained within the lower classes, their image was steadily developed by the integration of the idea of the demon lover and so the popular image of the vampire – as aristocratic lover – began to emerge. From here, as Punter and Byron state, 'No other monster has endured, and proliferated, in quite the same way – or been made to bear such a weight of metaphor. Confounding all categories, the vampire is the ultimate embodiment of transgression' (2003: 268). As they continue to analyse the metaphoric value of this creature, Punter and Byron make clear that the developmental trajectory of the vampire predominately aligns them with sexuality and seduction and, as a consequence, signifiers of repressed sexual desires: 'throughout the nineteenth century, the vampire functions to police the boundaries between "normal" and "deviant" sexuality with the narrative voice firmly positioned on the side of "normal"' (2003: 269–70).

These developmental qualities all manifest themselves, from the very start of *Hellraiser*, within the character of Frank Cotton. When the audience first see him, buying the puzzle box from an anonymous Oriental antique dealer, he is shown in partial shadow yet his clothes are sweat stained and filthy, his skin moist and dirty. Having struck a deal, Frank slides a bundle of notes across a table, with Barker cutting a close-up of Frank's hand – his fingernails are bitten and broken, with a thick layer of grime beneath each nail. His skin is tanned but the lines upon his hands are incised with dirt. The overall impression is of poverty if not peasantry.

This image of a filthy peasant is later contrasted during Julia's flashback to her to first encounter with Frank: opening the front door she is confronted with a handsome, cleanly shaven young man. He stands in the rain, his wet t-shirt clinging to his muscular body. Here, Frank appears as a sexually charged being, the emerging demon lover. He introduces himself as 'I'm Frank, I'm brother Frank.' Yet Julia stands still, seemingly transfixed by his appearance. He smiles and asks 'Well, can I come in or not?' (Fig. 2) Although seemingly innocuous, this line of dialogue makes the first explicit indication that Frank is

functioning as a vampire for, traditionally, a vampire cannot enter a house unless invited. This dialogue breaks his spell over Julia and she too smiles and says 'You're very welcome.' It is no coincidence that while Julia stands in the doorway looking at Frank she rests her right hand protectively upon her throat.

Fig. 2: Frank, the vampire, waits to be invited in

Once inside, Frank's seduction and then fornication with Julia – who, at this point in the narrative, is the virginal bride to be – functions as an expression of the vampire's sexual allure and prowess. The scenes of their adultery are seemingly blunt and a matter of fact as opposed to the romanticised view of sexual activity that the majority of films portray. This is possibly because this act of intercourse isn't sexually charged for Frank (where it obviously is for Julia) for he sees her as merely another sexual conquest, another cruel assault upon his weaker, older brother. It is worth noting that the scene also contains repressed elements of sadistic behaviour as Frank initiates the foreplay by producing a flick knife and cuts Julia's underwear away from her body. The blade, with its nickel sharp edge, catches the fading sunlight and with its pointed, penetrating end acts as a surrogate set of fangs, drawing together in one image the sexual aberrance that excites Frank with his suppressed role as a vampire.

Upon his bloody re-birth, Frank's vampiric qualities manifest themselves again. The first and most blatant indications lie in his constant request for more blood and the manner in which he 'absorbs' the blood of Julia's victims: he crawls over to their bodies and, pushing their heads forward, seemingly 'bites' the back of their necks in order to suck out their blood. A further indication as to Frank's vampiric state is more subtle and more prolonged throughout the narrative. As the audience learns more about Frank and his lifestyle, the sense of his peasant existence becomes more apparent and so suggests that although he may be a sexually transgressive seducer he amounts to still nothing more than the peasant vampire of Eastern European tradition. This interpretation is consolidated by Frank preying upon his own biological family – he first seduces Julia and has sexual relations with her. He later coerces her into committing murder and repays her not with sexual gratification but by murdering her for more blood. He also murders his own brother to satisfy his blood lust. And, as the film draws to an end, it is implied that he intends to seduce his cousin and then, more than likely, kill her too.

With its vampiric character and a narrative imbued with sexual transgression, Barker's *Hellraiser* has obvious parallels with Baker's *The Vampire Lovers*. In both narratives the vampire is a fundamentally evil creature whose preferences for sexual difference are made possible through their vampiric state. Emphasis is placed upon the seduction as much as the sexual act, lending to each film a subtle and perverse sense of the erotic. Here, sex is forbidden for such a consensual act is beyond the norms of accepted society. As the transgressor and the transgressed, the vampire is the arch seducer who facilitates the innocent's passage to their ambivalent desires.

With such qualities, Baker's film recalls the golden age of Hammer, where the Gothic tropes dominated the narrative and visual texture of each film. Barker's own relationship to this tradition and these films suggests an acknowledgement and the subtle possibility of influence. He has said of the Hammer films:

> 'Those were classic stories re-told for a new audience. They were very romantic movies. [Peter] Cushing's Baron Frankenstein is a classic Byronic romantic hero; he's a dashing and attractive character. Christopher Lee's Dracula has great sexual frisson… In Hammer's retelling, the colour, the slickness, the panache, moves the horror movie on, and I believe they are best viewed as Gothic adventures.' (Wells, 2002: 174–5)

It would seem with *Hellraiser* that Barker has absorbed and combined such qualities to create a reconfigured sense of Hammer's Gothic: his narrative is immensely romantic, albeit perversely so, for it is driven by love and desire whilst his antagonists, Frank and the Cenobites, become both 'dashing and attractive' for they seduce the audience with the possibilities they offer. Such qualities suggest, as Barker comments, 'a celebration of the monstrous and that can definitely be traced in the British Gothic sensibility. There is a romantic element in those monsters; a moral ambiguity that is very attractive' (ibid.).

FRANK AS WOUND

A further recurring element within Barker's work is the relationship between sex and violence, sex and the wound, and sex and death. These various combinations manifest themselves in Barker's typical aberrant fashion, simultaneously functioning as singular moments that shock but also as signifiers of meaning. Within his early literary works, this use of sex as device often signified the instance of transition where a character which lacked identity, personality, strength and courage is suddenly imbued with all of these qualities to the extent that sex and an accompanying 'injury' instigate a Rite of Passage.

Within *Hellraiser* Barker reconfigures these pairings and instead uses them to consolidate character traits. Given that Frank spends the majority of the film without his skin, he can be easily interpreted as a manifestation of the wound. This coupled with both his sexual needs and his propensity for violence aligns him with sex, violence and death, with the latter being compounded given that Frank has literally been brought back from the dead. In this respect, the Cenobites also function in a similar way for they too are physical manifestations of wound whose desires are fixated upon the expression of extreme sexuality and extremely violent acts.

Frank's relationship to these qualities are perhaps more pronounced because of the nature of his re-birth: as Julia stands alone in the attic remembering her first (and only) sexual encounter with Frank, her husband, Larry, is helping the removal men lift the marital bed up the stairwell. In a sequence of blatant and explicit cross-cuts, Barker visually positions the images of Frank thrusting into Julia with an image of Larry's hand moving back and forth and closer and closer to an exposed rusting nail. As Julia remembers the intensity of her orgasm, Larry's right hand catches on the nail. The rusted head of nail digs deep into his flesh and tears a gouge along his thumb. His scream of pain coincides with Julia's memory of pleasurable exaltation.

The scene concludes with Larry stumbling into the attic, holding his bleeding hand out to Julia as if he were a child. Without interrupting the flow of this scene, Barker cuts to an image of Larry's blood dripping onto the attic floorboards. It is from this accidental spillage of blood that Frank is re-born. This purely image-driven sequence makes explicit the connection between Frank and Barker's concept of the wound: the cross-cutting connects the sex act with the wound, suggesting that Larry's injury has sexual connotations. With this grotesque symbolic connection in place, Frank's birth is, literally, from the blood of a sexualised wound. Once again, the pleasurable act of sex is counter-balanced by violence and bloodshed. Whereas previously this correlation meant a positive progression for Barker's characters, within *Hellraiser* the relationship leads to the birth of the monster. It is perhaps not surprising then that this sequence is in itself monstrous – the moment when the rusty nail penetrates Larry's hand is brutally realistic and is shown in an explicit close-up whilst the sexual activity between Frank and Julia is, as previously mentioned, not one of a 'safe heterosexual' union but one that has sadistic and violent overtones.

Frank's actual re-birth is perversely remarkable: Larry's spilt blood is absorbed into the floorboards and it is from those single drops that Frank's heart, mind and body are reconstituted. The audience witnesses Frank's bodily reconstruction in explicit detail with the camera lingering upon the viscera of human organs steadily forming and connecting, the heart beating, the lungs expanding and contracting with each unsteady breath (Fig. 3). It is another grotesque and unnatural birth but Barker makes this sickening moment celebratory by placing a triumphant soundtrack over the image – instead of being repulsed by the imagery, the soundtrack encourages the audience to witness this re-birth as a glorious moment.

Fig. 3: Frank reborn

JULIA, THE MONSTROUS MOTHER

Julia is visually the least horrific of *Hellraiser*'s monsters. She functions more as a wicked stepmother to Kirsty's innocent stepdaughter. Yet her commitment to Frank and the consequential murders she commits for him make her equally as horrific as her lover and, to a certain extent, the Cenobites as well. Once again, Barker frames the horror of this character within the framework of sex and sexuality, using Julia's desire for further physical relations with Frank as the motivation for her crimes. Inherently involved in this is her posing as a high-class prostitute, a sexual cliché who trawls the midday bars looking for businessmen to seduce. Her charade hinges upon the fantasy that cliché implies for those drunken men, the promise that she will live out their desires.

The more Julia kills the more seductive she becomes, a transformation that Barker makes clear through the use of costume, styling and lighting: 'We did… things with the way Claire Higgins was made up, the way her hair was done and the way she was costumed to suggest that she was more beautiful the more she committed murder' (Floyd, 1987). Although these changes Barker describes are subtle, Julia's transformation from bland housewife to beautiful temptress again consolidates the narrative's preoccupation with combining beauty with violence (Fig. 4). It would seem, from the transformative effects that occur upon Julia, that the murders she is willingly committing are providing her the opportunity to literally become herself – the violence allows her a cathartic release from her role as a bored and repressed housewife and so instigates another of Barker's violently transformative moments. Her increased confidence as a murderer gives her an empowerment over males and becomes all the more charged by the fact that her sex and sexuality are the hook upon which men are drawn. The more plain businessmen she murders (which, in itself can be read as Julia repeatedly murdering representations of her boring husband Larry) the more sexually empowered she becomes. It is as if the more blood she spills the more she becomes Frank's equal. As a consequence of this, Barker's narrative implies that Julia and Frank are literally being made for one another.

THE FAMILY UNIT

*Fig. 4: Julia,
one seductive
murderer*

If the monstrous elements and graphic imagery were all taken away from *Hellraiser* then the narrative is reduced down to a family drama, one that is specifically focused upon the slow and steady collapse of a family unit. Examining the film from this perspective shunts the horrific elements to the very edges of the narrative and, as a consequence, they have very little motivating energy within the film. Instead, the character's motivations come from the acts they themselves instigate – Julia allows herself to be seduced by Frank while Frank simultaneously sees this seduction as merely another cynical sexual conquest. Larry moves back to England with Julia and into the ancestral home in the hope of reviving their failing marriage and to strengthen his relationship with his daughter. Yet Kirsty wants to be free of the family and begin to make her first step towards adult independence. Within this disparate family group lies a complex set of relationships that feed off each other and so, inextricably, draw each towards their narrative fates.

Considering *Hellraiser* as a family drama suggests that the film's heritage lies not within the Gothic or horror tradition but more within the 'Kitchen Sink' dramas of the British New Wave of the late 1950s-early 60s. It seems odd to suggest this for those films have no relationship at all to the horror genre for they explicitly explored the harsh reality of the working classes, identifying their struggles and their attempts to overcome them. Inherently involved in these dramas would be the considerable emphasis placed upon family life, where a notion of class and tradition still held sway and dictated the hierarchal nature of family relationships. A further trait was the friction between classes, where the working class would be placed in narrative conflict with members of the middle class. Here, contrasts between the poor and unskilled and the skilled and educated took precedence in order to create both a reflection of contemporary society as much as an ideological debate.

The central narrative of *Hellraiser* revolves around these very ideas. Perhaps the most obvious parallel comes from the relationship between Larry and Frank: constructed on opposites, Frank appears as a sexually liberated representation of the poor, unskilled and criminal element whilst Larry is sexually repressed and represents an ideal of a skilled and educated worker, a man who earns his money through the daily grind of white-collar work. This tension between them hardly ever physically manifests itself within the film but is clearly palpable via its mediation through Julia. Because of this, Julia becomes the crux of the narrative for she is the woman the brothers are ultimately struggling over. Julia's awareness of this situation only amplifies the opposition between the brothers – Frank's sexual prowess and rough masculinity only reinforce Larry's weakness and sexual immaturity. This set of oppositions places great emphasis on the dominating masculine force of the working classes, one that is violent and seductive, manipulative and unforgiving. In the face of such characteristics, the middle class is shown to be weak and shallow, blind to the realities of the situation and unable to cope with increasingly dire situations. Within Barker's sensibilities, the Kitchen Sink drama celebrates difference within a society yet allows neither group the opportunity to overpower the other. Consequently, those class signifiers are effectively removed from the narrative in order to allow the young, open-minded child to restructure the family and its position within society.

All of these elements are compounded by Barker's consistent use of realist tropes. The film begins by showing the dull and dreary world which Larry and Julia have moved into: Lodovico Street is a bland suburb in England with the house itself blurring into the surrounds as if it were a crumbling relic. Inside, the house is dark, all polished wood, settling dust and fading yellow wallpaper. It is, perhaps, a wry joke on Barker's part that once Larry and Julia begin to explore the house they come across a filthy, broken kitchen sink, crammed with plates and rotting food – an apt visual metaphor for the forthcoming narrative.

KIRSTY AND FRANK

Alongside his monstrous properties, Frank brings with him a deep sense of corruption. Like the vampire who contaminates with his bite, Frank contaminates with sex, sexuality and seduction. His first seductive act – seducing Julia – instigates the beginnings of both the Cotton family's collapse and the emergence of its aberrant qualities.

The corruption begins when Julia willingly engages in sexual congress with Frank. Instead of creating a sense of guilt within Julia (as might be expected) it instead generates a sense of longing. With Frank gone, all that is left is an empty void which Larry cannot fill. Instead, this void functions only to highlight his weakness and his failure as a husband and a lover. The relationship begins to disintegrate as Julia waits for the return of Frank for only he can fill the void he created.

Later, when Frank is partially formed, his corrupting qualities again to come to fore: having followed Julia to the family home, Kirsty sees her entering the house with another man. Investigating further she stumbles upon both the skinless Frank and Julia's latest victim. Kirsty staggers out onto the stairwell as Frank steps out towards her, his hands held out on an effort to try and calm her down: 'Kirsty, it's Frank. Uncle Frank.' She tries to move away from him but he takes hold of her and pushes her against the wall. 'You remember,' he hisses, 'come to Daddy.' Kirsty screams and manages to break free of Frank's grip and runs into the attic room where Frank corners her. As he walks slowly towards her his suggestive incestuous comments continue – 'You've grown. You're beautiful' – and he again takes hold of her (Fig. 5). Holding her against the wall, he pushes himself against her, forcing her head up with one of his fleshy fingers. 'There's nothing to be afraid of.

I bet you make your Daddy so proud, don't you, beautiful.' Kirsty tries to struggle free and whispers 'This isn't happening' to which Frank replies: 'I used to tell myself that. I tried to pretend I was dreaming all the pain but don't kid yourself. Some things have to be endured and that's what makes the pleasure so sweet.' Although referring to his experiences with the Cenobites, this last line of dialogue, coupled with his firm grip on Kirsty, also makes Frank's current intentions very clear – he intends to rape his niece and will, to all intents and purpose, not only enjoy it but also see it as another victory over his weak brother. Frank leans forward and tries to kiss Kirsty but she kicks him in the groin and manages to escape.

Fig. 5: The first incestuous advance

This injury and the intention of sexual assault have not been forgotten by Frank. As the film draws to an end, Barker positions Julia, Frank (who is now wearing his brother's skin) and Kirsty in a triangular formation at the bottom of the stairwell. Frank once again steps towards Kirsty with his hands held out and almost pleads with her: 'Stay with us. We can be happy here… Come to Daddy.' The moment is horrific for now Frank can have all that Larry has had and more for his suggestion is to create a normal, balanced family unit. Kirsty hesitates and for a moment so does Frank for he seems to genuinely believe that a family can be constructed with stepdaughter, stepmother and the monstrous uncle / lover, regardless of his incestuous intentions.

Realising that the man who stands before her is not her father, Kirsty tries to escape but is restrained by Julia. Frank grins, licking his lips as he takes out his flick knife and approaches Kirsty. They struggle and Kirsty manages to break free of Julia's grip just as Frank thrusts his knife toward her. The blade, its nickel sharp edge again catching the fading light, instead penetrates Julia's stomach. 'It's nothing personal' says Frank as he pushes the blade deeper into her.

The family drama concludes with Frank chasing Kirsty through the house and finally into the attic, his flick knife smeared with Julia's blood and held out before him. This final pursuit, coupled with the phallic nature of the flick knife, again suggests a sexual murder, a possible rape before death. Frank has already penetrated Julia with the knife and his intention is to do it again to Kirsty. In these final moments, all notions of the family, aberrant or not, have been contaminated and destroyed by Frank. Larry, the weak and helpless father, is dead and Julia, the wicked stepmother, is bleeding to death on the stairwell. All that remains is the Uncle hunting his niece. It seems appropriate then that the film should end with Frank finally meeting the Cenobites once more, with Kirsty barely escaping and 59 Lodovico Street, that haunted house of past, collapsing into nothing more than rubble.

Hellraiser ends as it began: Kirsty throws the Lament Configuration into a burning pyre only for it taken by a winged demon. Flying into the night sky, it carries the box back to the anonymous owner who once again sits at the dirty table and asks another unsuspecting customer 'What's your pleasure?' suggesting, perhaps predictably, a sequel.

Such was the success of *Hellraiser* that a sequel, *Hellbound: Hellraiser 2* (Tony Randel, 1988) was duly put into production. Barker's participation amounted to writing a story outline which took the story back up only days after the events of the first film. Featuring Kirsty and a resurrected Julia, the film delves deeper into the mythology of the Cenobites by entering Hell itself as Kirsty tries to free her murdered father. Whilst still retaining the stark and graphic qualities of the original, Hellbound offered a more aware and possibly caricatured version of the Lead Cenobite, now dubbed 'Pinhead' by his legion of fans. Regardless, audiences were still attracted to his exploits and subsequent sequels would follow and, with each, a commensurate decline in quality. Despite this the popularity of both *Hellraiser* and its central antagonist, Pinhead, remains to the extent that, at the time of writing, a Barker-sanctioned remake is seemingly underway.

ENDNOTES

[1] Within *Hellraiser* the Faust myth is evident in the relation between Frank and the Cenobites: by opening the Lament Configuration box, Frank unwittingly makes a deal with the Cenobites – they will show him the extremes of pleasure in return for his soul.

REFERENCES

Edwards, Philip. 'Hair-Raiser', *Crimson Celluloid*, No. 1, January 1998, *Revelations: The Official Clive Barker Resource* (http://www.cliverbarker.info.)[Accessed 03/03/08].

Floyd, Nigel. 'Clive Barker', *Samhain*, No. 4, July 1987, *Revelations: The Official Clive Barker Resource* (http://www.cliverbarker.info.)[Accessed 03/03/08].

Hellraiser (1987). Directed by Clive Barker [DVD], Europe: Anchor Bay Entertainment UK Ltd.

Howe, David J. '*Hellraiser*', Starburst, No. 110, October 1987, *Revelations: The Official Clive Barker Resource* (http://www.cliverbarker.info.)[Accessed 03/03/08]

Hurley, Kelly. 'British Gothic fiction, 1885–1930' pp. 189-207 in Hogle, Jerrold E. (ed.) *The Cambridge Companion to Gothic Fiction*, Cambridge: Cambridge University Press, 2002.

Le Blanc, Michelle and Odell, Colin. *Horror Films*, Hertfordshire: Pocket Essentials, 2001.

Punter, David and Byron, Glennis. *The Gothic*, London: Blackwell, 2003.

CHAPTER 6: MARY SHELLEY'S FRANKENSTEIN

ADAPTING FRANKENSTEIN

'British actor-director Kenneth Branagh, best known for his fearless and lucid film
adaptations of Shakespeare, has at last given us the real Mary Shelley's Frankenstein,
mating a literate, dynamic screenplay with a brilliant cast that stars Robert De Niro as the
Creature, Branagh himself as Victor Frankenstein, the doctor obsessed with reclaiming life,
and Helena Bonham Carter as his beloved Elizabeth.' (Branagh, 1994)

Within any critical text that is concerned with Branagh's adaptation of *Mary Shelley's
Frankenstein* (1818), the legitimacy of adaptation is commented upon. For a novel that
has been adapted so many times for television, film and theatre it is not surprising that
academics and critics should be so preoccupied with this aspect of the film. This is
perhaps even more the case because Branagh and his producers Francis Ford Coppola,
James V. Hart and John Veitch, have named their film *Mary Shelley's Frankenstein*. By merely
placing the author's name within the title (as Coppola did with his *Bram Stoker's Dracula*,
1992) it suggests that this will be a faithful screen adaptation. But what does this mean
– a faithful screen adaptation?

When translating a narrative from one medium to another – from a classic novel to a contemporary film – there are going to be inevitable compromises. These may be due to practical elements (with the budget being the obvious obstacle in any part of the adaptation process) but is more grounded in the nature of the audience. The Creature of *Frankenstein* is as universally recognised as much as the narrative he inhabits. Both have been visualised many, many times, in many, many different ways, in both serious and comic contexts[1]. All these years of cultural representation of one character and one narrative build up a universally recognised set of conventions: the Creature must be made of mutilated flesh, his intelligence slow and stupid; his creator must be an obsessed madman aided by a hunchback; the Creature's birth must take place within a castle during a raging storm; and, as the narrative unfolds, vengeance is wreaked but, by the end, the Creature is successfully destroyed, usually by fire. These components are culturally understood to be synonymous not only with Shelley's *Frankenstein* but with the cinematic adaptations of *Frankenstein*: so popular is this narrative and so potent are its images, that cinema has managed to successfully usurp the role of the original to the extent that it has consumed it and replaced it as the narrative's defining image.

Within Branagh's version, there is an attempt to rectify this situation and present, as literally as possible, a close adaptation of Shelley's original novel. This, in itself, is a grand undertaking, and one that was not lost on Branagh ('I hope Mary Shelley would at least approve of the attempt' [1994: 29]). Gone is the clichéd image of the Creature as a slow, lumbering idiot. He is now a grotesquely fabricated man, but one with intelligence and emotion. Gone too is the depiction of Victor Frankenstein as a crazed megalomaniac, replaced with a man traumatised by the death of his mother and fixated on the eradication of death. This man no longer needs an assistant for he is embroiled in arcane work. He is a loner, isolating himself from society in the hope of creating life. As well as returning the characters to Shelley's origins, Branagh, Production Designer Tim Harvey and Art Director Martin Childs attempt to construct a believable period setting in which to place the narrative with the world in which the characters inhabit built in accordance with historic accuracy. This attention to detail was central to the Creature's birthing apparatus. As Harvey comments:

> '*Since Shelley gives no details at all about how Frankenstein actually achieves the creation, we based our designs on what would have been possible for a scientist of that period to use in the way of equipment. We did a great deal of research on what was available, and the result was a very low-tech set-up.*' (Branagh, 1994: 67)

For all their attempts at faithful adaptation, Branagh, Lady and Darabont still made a number of significant changes. These differences shift the film from an honest, literal adaptation and push towards more of a revisionist visual text. Of the changes the director and screenwriters made, the most important include:

- The expansion of the role played by Elizabeth.

- The explicit reference to motherhood and its relationship to Shelley's biography.

- The death of Victor's mother.

- The reanimation of Elizabeth / Justine's combined corpse.

These changes – and in some cases entirely new additions – place an emphasis upon the role and representation of women. In her essay, 'Feminist sympathies versus masculine backlash: Kenneth Branagh's *Mary Shelley's Frankenstein*', Heidi Kaye sees these additions as a contradiction, undermined by both the narrative and the events that take place within it: 'In *Mary Shelley's Frankenstein*, Kenneth Branagh attempts to create a *Frankenstein* for the 1990s. On one thematic level, the film offers a feminist interpretation of the text by stressing the issues surrounding motherhood and women's roles… Yet on another level, Branagh's version recreates the gendered polarities which feminist readings of the novel argue are undermined by Shelley' (1996: 57).

By trying to update (read as 'modernise' for a more equality driven society) the roles occupied by women, Branagh actually undermines his agenda of authenticity, for the women in the novel are not wholly central to the narrative – only Victor and his Creature should occupy that prime space. Although Branagh's expansion of the roles of Elizabeth and depiction of Victor's mother do raise interesting critical readings, they also create an unsettling division between the sexes, resulting in the self sacrifice of the women in an effort to gain their independence.

Regardless of this, Branagh should be applauded for his attempt at trying to create a new and contemporary *Frankenstein* by paying attention to the original source. It is a dark and painful story of obsession and the limits of man's willingness to explore. As such it is a narrative which needs to be told with the clarity of realism because its potential for metaphor and meaning still holds value in our increasingly technological society.

THE STAR

Of his choice to cast Robert De Niro as the Creature, director Branagh said:

'Most people… are really only aware of the Creature through comic books or the Munsters *or the* Addams Family. *I think that to overcome such preconceptions, we had to cast an actor of power and stature. There should be something in the very casting, the very mention of the person's name that would intrigue people as to how this great actor would interpret this classic screen role.'* (1994: 21–2)

Initially, De Niro's casting seems to be against type for the role of the Creature can be interpreted as somewhat of a departure from this actor's evolving body of work: celebrated for his commitment to the Method school of acting, De Niro is renowned for his intense portrayal of troubled, conflicted and often violent characters – Travis Bickle (*Taxi Driver*, Martin Scorsese, 1976), Jake La Motta (*Raging Bull*, Scorsese, 1980), Rodrigo

Mendoza (*The Mission*, Roland Joffé, 1986) and Neil McCauley (*Heat*, Michael Mann, 1995) – yet this description adequately describes the Creature, for his psychology is preoccupied with the conflicting feelings and anxieties over his origins. From this conflict, harmony and understanding, violence and retribution are all borne and fused into one emotional being. As a consequence, the Creature is, by the narrative's end, no different to many of the other characters De Niro has so eloquently played before: many are searching for some sense of understanding in a world which they no longer comprehend. They feel isolated and rejected by the world and attempt to re-establish themselves within it by committing perhaps well intentioned but ultimately violent and destructive acts. Most are bound by personal codes of honour and will, if necessary, die for such strictures.

It is these qualities, these very attributes, which define the Creature's central narrative for he is a being that is rejected by a world he clearly cannot comprehend. His attempts to peacefully integrate himself into society result in further rejection and humiliation, leaving him with only one course of action – to adhere to his personal codes ('I keep my promises…') and exact a violent revenge upon his very maker. Interpreting the Creature in this way implies that, within Branagh's adaptation at least, the Creature is quite literally a product of society. His birth is instigated by the urge to advance science whilst his development from a new born to adult is a consistent trauma of rejection, from his 'biological' father to those he later encounters.

VICTOR FRANKENSTEIN

Victor's (Kenneth Branagh) narrative is driven by the father / son relationship: initially this is with his biological father, Alphonse (Ian Holm) and then, when Victor has left home to go to Ingolstadt University, he replaces the biological father with a surrogate father, Professor Waldham (John Cleese). Upon successfully animating the dead flesh of his creation, Victor himself takes on the role of the symbolic father.

All three fathers are unified by their intellects and their innate capacity for science. Their quests for further knowledge are initially successful but, ultimately, their pursuit of knowledge and the application of that knowledge can only lead to death. For all his skills as a physician, Alphonse cannot save his wife during childbirth; whilst attempting to inoculate the poor against cholera, Waldham is accused of spreading the disease and is then murdered; and Victor – for all the success he has in reanimating the dead – fails to realise that creating life is only part of the experiment, that the rest is to support and nurture that resurrected life. As a consequence, Victor's rejection of his 'child' results in the death of Alphonse, his brother, William (Ryan Smith), his friend, Justine (Trevyn McDowell) and his wife, Elizabeth (Helena Bonham Carter).

Victor's ambition to erase death and so create 'a being that won't grow old, that won't sicken, a being that will be more intelligent than us, more civilised than us' is indeed heroic but fundamentality flawed. It is an essential and inescapable fact that once we are born that part of our destiny is an inevitable death. Instead of attempting to sustain or prolong a healthy life, Victor wants to be a God, to have the power to create life. This desire provides an accurate analysis of his character: he is a passionate and driven individual who is, to use Branagh's description, 'a dangerously sane man' (1994: 17), one whose strength lies in a misguided conviction that he is 'trying to do the right thing' (ibid.)

Although Victor has successfully usurped the role of God by fashioning a life with his mortal hands, perhaps his real crime is that of immediately rejecting the Creature. This theme, as Branagh says, 'of parental abandonment is tremendously strong, and we tried to give Victor a moment where he is faced with what this means' (1994: 19).

As the film draws to a close, Victor is given the opportunity to explain to the Creature why he rejected him: sitting opposite each other in an ice cavern, the son talks to the father, asking him who he is made of. Were they good people or bad people? Why did he give him emotions if he were not going to teach him how to use them? Does he have a soul? And, finally, the Creature asks 'Did you ever consider the consequences of your actions? You gave me life then left me to die. Who am I?' There is a pause then Victor answers 'I don't know'.

The very fact that Victor creates a being and then immediately rejects it signifies an inability to bear the responsibility of not just being a surrogate parent but also rejecting the responsibility of creating: to create life is only part of the task Victor sets out for himself for he consistently fails to realise that his creation needs parental care and a safe environment in which to grow. The film subtly hints at this through the depiction of Victor's own family life. The Frankenstein home is shown as a safe, warm and loving environment, clean and protective yet the 'home' of the Creature is, as Shelley describes in her novel, 'a workshop of filthy creation' (Shelley, 1831: 55). Within the *mise-en-scène* of the film the workshop is a dark and dismal space, and although what little light filters through is soft and gold, it is still a space in which unholy work is being completed. It is no coincidence that the Creation and Victor finally meet to talk over family matters at Mont Blanc – a cold, desolate and empty space.

The scene in the ice cavern is a pivotal moment in the relationship between Victor and the Creature for the Creature – whom Victor has continually assumed to be monstrous – demonstrates his innate humanity by describing his self awareness and his understanding of the world into which he has been 'born'. Instead of being an evil being, the Creature is depicted as gentle, articulate and considerate: he offers Victor the warmth of his fire; he speaks eloquently of his life and how he desires an equal. He expresses the need to love and to be loved, even if that is from another reanimated being.

The Creature's eloquence is in contrast to Victor who, throughout the conversation, remains cold and distanced and, at times, inarticulate. He is surprised his creation can speak and the implication that it can learn. His disgust becomes evident when he described the creature's mortal body as 'Materials. Nothing more' and his suggestion that the Creature's capacity to learn comes merely from 'trace memories in the brain'. Victor's dialogue suggests a fear of what he has himself created and, once again, he is unable to see the potential the Creature has. Instead of embracing his 'son' he once again tries to reject him through denying his ability to learn, to understand and, perhaps more importantly, to feel emotion at a powerful level. It would seem, at least in this scene, that the creation is far more humane than his creator.

Within moments of his birth, the Creature is visually and verbally identified as the Other: as Victor looks upon his creation, he writes of his failure within his journal, commenting that the Creature has 'massive birth defects… malfunctional and pitiful, dead'. Later, when the Creature pursues Victor through the laboratory, Professor Krempe says (in voice over): 'How was it pieced together? With bits of thieves? Bits of murderers? Evil stitched to evil stitched to evil.' Such dialogue not only anticipates the audience's first full sighting of the Creature but specifically constructs the Creature as the product of sinful man: his physical being is a construct of evil men whilst the very fact that the Creature lives and breathes is a blasphemy. Herein lies the Creature's symbolic potential, for he is simultaneously a positive expression of humanity's pursuit to better itself but also a warning to the question of how far humanity is willing to go in the name of 'progress'.

This aspect of the Creature is, to a great extent, shifted onto Victor. This displacement constructs a sense of timelessness within the narrative, for the metaphoric values of both Victor and the Creature enable a historically grounded narrative to be aligned with a contemporary audience: the medical profession's constant quest to cure disease and sustain life is now coupled with technological advances that suggest life can be continued or even created from the parts of others – blood transfusions, organ donation and replacement, IVF treatment and, inevitably, cloning can all be paralleled with Victor's rigorous pursuit of scientific conquest. In the introduction to his book about the film, Branagh places great emphasis upon this interpretation:

'For me, the lasting power of the story lay in its ability to dramatise a number of moral dilemmas. The most obvious one is whether brilliant men of science should interfere in matters of life and death. Today's newspapers are littered with such dilemmas… We can all see these developments taking place now. It's now an imaginable step to prevent people from dying.' (1994: 17)

Branagh continues this theme, but from a more positive perspective:

'We hope audiences today may find parallels with Victor today in some amazing scientist who might be an inch away from curing AIDS or cancer, and needs to make some difficult decisions. Without this kind of investigative bravery, perhaps there wouldn't have been some of the advances we've had in the last hundred years.' (1994: 19)

THE BIRTH OF THE CREATURE

The *mise-en-scène* of Victor's laboratory is not so much a 'workshop of filthy creation' (Shelley, 1831: 55) but more a combination of sexual symbols: the womb in which the Creature is placed is a large copper coffin filled with amniotic fluids. Suspended above this are large testicular bags, each writhing with electric eels, surrogates for sperm. From these bags protrudes a blatant phallic symbol, a large hollow tube. Once Victor has placed the Creature inside the tomb-womb, he penetrates its head, body and feet with conducting needles and then 'enters' the womb by forcing the hollow tube into it. As the sequence reaches its climax, Victor releases the sperm-eels down the tube to 'fertilise' the body of the Creature with electric current (Fig. 1). The whole scene is, as Branagh says, 'full of sexual imagery' (1994: 20) that positions Victor not necessarily as the creator but more the symbolic unification of Mother and Father. Within this one scene he functions

as both parents, operating the surrogate male and female reproductive organs in order to create a new life. This sexually-charged reading immediately suggests that Victor is not only usurping the role of God but also that of Woman and so potentially expressing a deep anxiety over both reproduction and birth.

Fig. 1: The tomb-womb and scientific male genitals

This masculine anxiety over birth makes further connections with British science fiction. Ridley Scott's *Alien* (1979) is the most explicit manifestation of this concern as its narrative set-piece is literally (and somewhat grotesquely) a man giving birth: crew member Kane (John Hurt) is 'sexually' attacked by an alien organism which impregnates him by forcing a phallic tube down his throat. Although this creature dies, the seed inside Kane grows and, when ready to be born, the infant creature chews its way out of the man's stomach. Although this may be the narrative's most blatant scene of birth anxiety, the film itself is heavily coded throughout with the imagery of reproduction. Like Victor's laboratory in *Mary Shelley's Frankenstein*, the *mise-en-scène* of the space vessel *Nostromo* is a complex construction of womb-like interiors, all connected with corridors that function like birth canals, whilst the various doorways and hatches all take on a vaginal quality. The sexualised nature of this environment is consolidated by the naming of the ship's computer – Mother. Within *Alien* the female body is represented as a clean and safe space but one that is also open to violation. Within *Mary Shelley's Frankenstein* this is inverted as both the female body and its reproductive capabilities are externalised, made of copper and steel and integrated with the male reproductive organs into one asexual construct.

THE CREATURE

Fig. 2: The Creature

When the audience finally does get to see the Creature, it is truly hideous – the slack and diseased skin, the grotesquely congealed scars running the length of his face, his cleft lips – all of which initially seem to contradict Victor's vision of designing '…a being that will not grow old or sicken, one that will be stronger than us, better than us, one that will be more intelligent than us, more civilised than us' (Fig. 2). But, as the film progresses it becomes apparent that Victor has indeed achieved his goal for the Creature demonstrates both physical *and* emotional strength, a balanced intelligence and greater sense of civility than those who surround him.

Almost immediately after he has been rejected by his creator, the Creature is victimised and stereotyped by a range of minor characters: escaping the laboratory, the Creature conceals his deformed face beneath a heavy cowl and wanders the plague-stricken streets, finally coming upon a market place. Without realising he is stealing, the Creature picks up a loaf of bread and takes a bite. The stall vendor challenges him but when she sees his face she screams. The Creature drops the loaf and tries to run but is stopped by a man who pulls at the cowl, revealing his deformed features further. The stall vendor has now taken up a knife and starts to shout 'He's the cholera, He's the one been spreadin' the plague!' The people in the market suddenly turn into an angry mob, throwing stones at the Creature and hitting him with staffs as he tries to escape. The stereotype is obvious: a hideously malformed man must be the source of the epidemic. Instead of running away from the threat, the people quickly descend into mob mentality and attack the innocent Creature.

This sequence contains two further incidents: whilst trying to escape, the Creature demonstrates his immense strength by overturning a cart laden with barrels and then, when pushing someone out of the way, he does so with such force that the person is killed. This strength is again another negative indicator, that the Creature's physicality is not something to be admired (as it would be within a protagonist) but, like the Creature's physical deformities, something to be feared. The scene ends with the Creature escaping by, ironically, concealing himself amongst a cart loaded with the corpses of cholera victims.

These brief scenes immediately establish for the fictional characters and the audience that the Creature is the 'Monster'. Yet, as the narrative progresses, Branagh makes every effort to undermine this stereotyping to the extent that when the Creature and Victor finally meet in the ice cavern the Creature has become a countertype: he has shown a capacity for empathy and kindness by using his immense strength to unearth the vegetables beneath the frozen soil to give them to Felix (Mark Hadfield) and his family. He demonstrates intelligence by learning to read, to speak articulately and to express himself. He learns to play the recorder, he understands and enjoys beauty, and longs for an equal to share his life with. The implication of these learning experiences is that the Creature has overcome his difference to the extent that he becomes a sympathetic character, one who has a greater understanding of life, feeling and emotion than any of the other characters in the film.

By the narrative's end the Creature understands humanity's deep unkindness to each other to such an extent that when asked by Captain Walton (Aidan Quinn) to join the crew of the *Nevsky* (hence a final acceptance for who he is and not what he is) and return home with them, he simply replies 'I am done with Man.' By saying this, the Creature implies he understands that his acceptance into society may be no more than tolerance, that the stereotype will always exist no matter how much he undermines it. At a deeper level this dialogue could also imply a greater personal understanding to the extent that he accepts that he is an unholy creature and so commits suicide by immolating himself within Victor's burning funeral pyre.

THE DEATH OF THE MOTHER

Of all the changes Branagh and his script writers made to Shelley's original narrative, the most significant lies with the death of Caroline (Cherie Lunghi), Victor's mother and the expanding role of Elizabeth. Within the novel, Caroline successfully nurses Elizabeth through the Scarlet Fever only to then die of the disease herself. In Branagh's adaptation events from Shelley's life are coherently integrated into the narrative.

Mary Wollstonecraft Shelley was born in London 30 August 1797. An only child, both her parents were educated people and, at the time of her birth, established writers. Her mother, Mary Wollstonecraft, was a leading early feminist, whilst her father, William Godwin, was a noted philosopher. Their marriage took place five months before their daughter's birth but was tragically cut short as Mary would die of complications only ten days after the birth. Her death would have profound and traumatic consequences for her only child – it would not only leave her daughter to grow up without a mother but it would, perversely, set in motion the very beginnings of *Frankenstein*[2].

Instead of allowing his Caroline to die of a disease, Branagh draws upon these biographical events and within his adaptation Caroline functions as a metaphor for Shelley's own mother. Mary's and Caroline's death is fixed as a consequence of birth and so not only successfully aligns the fictional depiction with biographical fact but also sets out the film's understanding of birth – instead of being a powerful life affirming event, birth is grotesquely aligned with mortality (Fig. 3). Because of this, Branagh depicts Caroline's death in a truly horrific fashion: wearing a white but blood splattered gown, she writhes in a birthing chair. Her legs are splayed open, her grip on the chair's handles so tight her knuckles are white. She screams as her maid, Mrs. Moritz (Celia Imrie), mops her brow. Her husband kneels between her legs, his naked torso also splattered in blood. The camera continually spins around these three characters, its unsettling motion conveying

the distress of the moment. Alphonse, husband, father and physician, is paralysed by his wife's pain – 'the baby,' he says, 'is in the wrong position. I cannot proceed…' but his wife intervenes decisively: 'Cut me. Save the baby.' With an anguished scream, he begins to thrust his scalpel forward but Branagh cuts away. The audience has seen all they need to see.

Fig. 3: The death of the mother

Within the context of the forthcoming narrative, the death of the mother has a dual purpose for it highlights the failure of the Father whilst simultaneously functioning as the incident which sets Victor on his God-like quest to create life: upon hearing the first cries of William, his new born brother, Victor approaches the main stairwell only to see his father stumbling down the steps. He holds his blood drenched hands out before him. 'I killed my wife'[3] he says. He takes another step down. 'I did everything I could,' he murmurs, 'I did all I could.' He then collapses, sobbing into his bloody palms. Victor looks down at him in painful understanding. His father, described by Elizabeth only moments before as 'the finest doctor in Geneva', has failed.

In these two scenes, masculinity and patriarchy are undermined by the unpredictability of Nature and the strength of women. As good a doctor as he may be Alphonse cannot control the processes and complications of birth. He must stand on the outside of the female body and watch as it undergoes its own natural course. He is reduced to a scientific spectator, an immobilised viewer. In a tangential way, this suggests that Alphonse understands that his superior medical skill can only extend so far and that, inevitably in this situation, his role as doctor will be eventually reduced to the moral dilemma of whose life he should save. And, once confronted with this decision, he collapses, sobbing and refusing to look at his wife. His weakness comes from compromise and the inability to make a rationale choice. This collapse of skilled masculinity is paralleled by strong femininity for it is Caroline who makes the choice. It is her life and she takes control of it by deciding to sacrifice herself so that her son may live. It is a choice which positions the female as strong, capable and independent. It is also a choice which will have resonance later in the film, for the reanimated Elizabeth will also have to make the choice between life and death.

ELIZABETH

Branagh states that 'It was important to me to have a very strong woman's role… I wanted Elizabeth and Victor to be two equal partners, utterly entwined from the beginning. These two people were absolutely meant to be together' (1994: 6). To do this, screenwriters Lady and Darabont expanded Elizabeth's role, presenting her as a character more in line with contemporary women than the woman Shelley depicts in her novel. There she is weak and ineffectual, particularly when she attempts to free Justine from her death sentence. She is more a woman bound to the house and the requisite duties such a woman should perform. She is, in effect, a woman who is representative of her time. Lady and Darabont attempt to modernise their Elizabeth but the constraints of the narrative potentially confuse this representation: although their version of Elizabeth is strong and independent she is still bound to a mode of actions that rendered her ineffectual and equate her with domesticity. Elizabeth goes to Ingolstadt in an effort to rescue Victor from both his work and the cholera epidemic but is unsuccessful. Victor's desire for his work (or the depth of his trauma) overpowers his sense of love for her. Later, when Justine is dragged to the city walls to be hung, Elizabeth can only stand (with Victor) and cry out. It is worth noting that Victor offers Elizabeth the chance to join him in Ingolstadt as his wife, to which she replies: 'I want nothing more than anything else in the world to be your wife… but as long as you are away, I belong here. I want to make this house live again. I want to make this a great home for our children. And now you must go and do the great things you need to do.' This dialogue not only locates Elizabeth to a role that is, in effect, a housewife but it also implies a certain sense of subordination to (the male) Victor – it is he who must go out into the world and stake his claim, not both of them together in equal partnership.

Countering this is Branagh's interpretation of Elizabeth:

> 'Elizabeth's response to the family tragedies is much different than [Victor's]… She's obsessed about her family, is someone who understands the value of what it can mean to be head of a household, and indeed wants to replace the great gap caused by the loss of the mother. She's someone who has a capacity to enjoy, to live in the present, to appreciate the small details of life.' (1994: 25)

In this respect Elizabeth becomes a mirror of Victor – and so an equal of sorts – as both are preoccupied with the idea of the family and the urge to sustain that important unity. Victor satisfies these needs through attempting to resolve the trauma of his mother's death while Elizabeth seeks a more immediate and effective response – to deal with the death by rebuilding the family unit through marriage and the birth of grandchildren. It is interesting to note that both attempt to heal the family injuries through birth – Victor tries to usurp death through a process of arcane birth whilst Elizabeth merely wants to bear his children.

Perhaps more troubling is Elizabeth's potential status as a gift /object: (Fig. 4) Shelley's novel places more emphasis upon this than Branagh's adaptation does. Shelley writes: 'I have a pretty present for my Victor' where as in Branagh's film Victor is told by

Fig. 4: Elizabeth, the gift

his mother to '…think of her as your own sister. You must look after her. And be kind to her. Always.' Equality is clearly implied yet when Elizabeth is killed by the Creature and consequently resurrected by Victor her status as object (albeit an object of affection) is brought to the fore.

As he promised, the Creature is with Victor on his wedding night. Entering into the Frankenstein house, he murders Elizabeth. Overcome with grief, Victor takes Elizabeth's corpse to his laboratory and without emotion saws off her head, hands and feet. These appendages are then grafted onto Justine's body[4] and successfully reanimated (Fig. 5). Sitting her down, Victor dresses her in her wedding gown, and slips her wedding ring back onto her finger as he repeatedly asks Elizabeth to say his name. She instead responds to the sound of her own name. Victor helps her up and then places her hands on his shoulders so that they may dance. This brief moment is interrupted by the Creature who enters the laboratory and looks upon the resurrected Elizabeth, saying 'She's beautiful.' Elizabeth releases Victor and stumbles over to the Creature. Scared of losing

Fig. 5: Elizabeth, the monstrous creation

her again, Victor keeps asking her to say his name, which she finally manages to do. The Creature and Victor both take hold of Elizabeth and a struggle ensues, culminating in Elizabeth breaking free of their grasp. Staggering towards a table, Elizabeth picks up a kerosene lamp and smashes it over her head, showering her body in flames.

This scene is, as Heidi Kaye suggests, another example of Victor's selfish and single-minded pursuits: 'It is not surprising that it is to the Creature that [Elizabeth] goes to in this scene. It is he who has been calling her name and telling her she's beautiful, whereas Victor has been self-centredly asking her to remember him, not herself' (1996: 59). Kaye follows this with the comment upon Elizabeth's suicide: 'She wants no part in these men's games with life and death, and she refuses to be possessed by either of them; she creates her own destiny' (1996: 60).

Her self-immolation connects with the death of Caroline and the death of the Creature. With Victor dead and no equal to keep his company, the Creature commits suicide by embracing the flames of Victor's funeral pyre. Each of these three deaths is instigated by the individual, with each one choosing to die rather than to live in a traumatised state. Of the three, Elizabeth's death is most tragic for she is depicted as being without control, as being unable to exist independently and freely of Victor – her lover, her husband and now her creator. All that she strove for in her life – family harmony, happiness and a certain equality and independence – have been taken away by the resurrecting act.

Elizabeth's suicide generates a further reading, one that is clearly articulated by John Rieder in his critical text 'A filthy type: The motif of the fecal child in *Mary Shelley's Frankenstein*':

'…*Branagh gives the plot over… to the dynamics of heterosexual rivalry. His Victor actually creates the female companion but of course he does so for his own benefit, not that of his creature. When the resurrected Elizabeth chooses self-immolation over being made into the stakes of the struggle between Victor and the Creature, she no doubt represents a feminist resistance to the heterosexual / homosocial economy they are enacting*' (Rieder, 2001: 30).

Rieder's analysis suggests that Elizabeth does finally become a contemporary female for she rejects her role as object, albeit through death. This final defiant act of independence is coded as tragic because Elizabeth has to die in order for her independence to be instigated and maintained. Victor's selfish nature again consumes this action for instead of blaming himself for the loss of Elizabeth (on both occasions) he again blames the Creature and swears to kill him. Perhaps the real tragedy of this film is not the rejection of the monster or Elizabeth's death but the consequences of Victor's consistent blindness to the needs of others.

ENDNOTES

[1] Films include *Frankenstein* (James Whale, 1931), *Abbott and Costello meet Frankenstein* (Charles Barton, 1948), *Young Frankenstein* (Mel Brooks, 1974), *The Bride* (Franc Roddam, 1985), *The Monster Squad* (Fred Dekker, 1987) and *Frankenstein Unbound* (Roger Corman, 1990).

[2] 'Shelley's own experience of losing her first child within two weeks of its birth (compounded later by the death of another of her children) and the horrific dream of its revival ("Dream that my little baby came to life again; that it had only been cold and that we rubbed it before the fire, and it lived. Awake and find no baby. I think about the little thing all day. Not in good spirits") have [also] been read into the novel's concern's for non-reproductive creation and / or reanimation of the dead.' (Kaye, 1996: 58)

[3] It is worth noting that the father, Alphonse, kills his wife while his son, Victor, resurrects his dead wife. Regardless of this, both women meet the same narrative fate – death.

[4] This is an aberrant union for Victor has grafted Elizabeth's head, hands and feet onto Justine's torso. This merging of body parts has a perverse psychological quality for the physical union of the two women literally means that Victor gets to have both women – Elizabeth and Justine – simultaneously.

This connection of bodies and minds can also be extended to Professor Waldhman – Victor takes out Waldham's brain and, ironically, inserts it into the mutilated body of his murderer.

REFERENCES

Branagh, Kenneth. *Mary Shelley's Frankenstein – the Classic Tale of Terror Reborn on Film*, New York: Newmarket Press, 1994.

Kaye, Heidi, 'Feminist sympathies versus masculine backlash: Kenneth Branagh's *Mary Shelley's Frankenstein*' in Cartmell, Deborah, Hunter, I.Q., Kaye, Heidi and Whelehan, Imelda (eds), *Pulping Fictions*, Chicago: Pluto Press, 1996.

Mary Shelley's Frankenstein (1994). Directed by Kenneth Branagh [DVD], Europe: Columbia Tristar Home Entertainment.

Rieder, John, 'A filthy type – the motif of the fecal child in *Mary Shelley's Frankenstein*', pp. 24-31 in *Gothic Studies*, Vol. 3, Issue 1, April 2001.

CHAPTER 7: 28 DAYS LATER

GENRE

Placing *28 Days Later* (Danny Boyle, 2002) within a genre category is problematic. Given that this book is concerned with contemporary British horror cinema, the film must, by definition, be considered part of this tradition. Yet, scriptwriter Alex Garland refers to *28 Days Later* as a science fiction film (Newman, 2007). As its creator, Garland's view of the film's genre classification deserves respect, yet in terms of film and genre study, *28 Days Later* lacks the essential prerequisite conventions of the science fiction genre: it is not obviously set in the future, there are no extra-terrestrial elements to the film nor does the narrative take place in outer space or upon another planet. It is instead set in contemporary Britain, and advanced technological devices, space ships, transporter systems and lasers are all absent. Lacking these essential visual signifiers, the only two potential connections between the film and the science fiction genre is the catastrophic consequences of the 'Rage' virus and the sources that influenced Garland whilst he was writing the script. The majority of these influential texts – most notably John Wyndham's *The Day of the Triffids* (1951) – are considered to be classics of literary science fiction, particularly within the sub-genre of British post-apocalyptic fiction.

Post-apocalyptic fiction is preoccupied with the near destruction of civilisation through some terrible event, be that nuclear war, viral outbreak, plague or natural disaster. Although apocalyptic texts have existed for many decades, this sub-genre achieved significance after the Second World War as the general public became aware of the possibility of national and global destruction through nuclear attack. These fictions fed into those fears, exploring the possibility of survival in a world irreversibly changed overnight. Allegorically, the post-apocalyptic story alerts the reader to the negative consequence of scientific advancement and reminds them that we have, through such advancements, brought about the means of our own destruction. Whilst American fiction dealt with this in terms of the fantastic, English authors took a typically bleak British approach to the situation and presented their fictions as realistically, and as pessimistically, as possible (*The Last Man* [Mary Shelley, 1826], *The War of the Worlds* [H. G. Wells, 1898], *The Chrysalids* [John Wyndham, 1955] and *On the Beach* [Neville Shute, 1957], for example). Within their narratives, survival is a constant struggle, the landscape desolate or reclaimed by nature and man's actions reduced to the necessities of survival. In many ways, *28 Days Later* is, like *The Quatermass Xperiment*, clearly part of this sub-genre, particularly in relation to the intensely bleak realism both Garland and director Danny Boyle strive for within the narrative. Yet, even with these connections in place, the relationship between the film and science fiction remains tenuous.

Instead, it can be argued that *28 Days Later* rests more comfortably within the horror genre for it contains a significant number of the genre's tropes: the basic premise of the narrative is typical of most horror films in that it is concerned with an isolated group of people who are struggling against an overwhelming threat. As Odell and Le Blanc state in their book *Horror Films* (2001): 'the basic structural premise of the horror film is to show the restoration or reconstruction of an order in a portrayed society' and conclude that 'the reconstruction of order does not necessarily mean that the new world is any better than the one that preceded it and is often far worse but its alteration and the process of reconstruction is what provides the genre's basic narrative drive' (2001: 8).

This underlying narrative structure of horror films functions on Todorov's theory of equilibrium. His theory argues that within certain narratives, the fictional environment begins in a state of equilibrium. An incident then occurs which disrupts this sense of balance. A series of events then follow which result in the restoration of the equilibrium or an altered version of it. Because of this return to a similar state, Todorov implies that narratives are not necessarily linear but circular and that this return indicates a transformative change within certain characters. Taking the whole narrative of *28 Days Later* into account, it can be seen that Garland's script is essentially Todorovian in its principles: normality is in balance until the accidental release of the Rage virus. As the survivors move through the desolate landscape they are effectively in the process of re-establishing the old equilibrium with the narrative concluding with a two-fold restoration of balance: Jim (Cillian Murphy), Selena (Naomie Harris) and Hannah (Megan Burns) have formed a family unit within the safety of the countryside whilst the passing foreign jet implies the contagion has been contained within Britain. In addition to this, the narrative's circularity is enforced by the protagonist as the story begins with Jim recovering from an injury (a road accident) and ends with him recovering from an injury (a gunshot wound).

As previously stated one of the few connections between *28 Days Later* and the horror genre is the narrative threat: from the opening exposition, it is assumed that the Rage virus has been created for use as a biological weapon. This content draws parallels with *The Quatermass Xperiment* and *Mary Shelley's Frankenstein* for all three films contain elements of science fiction but are more preoccupied with the horrific consequence of unchecked scientific experimentation. Odell and Le Blanc suggest that there are four types of monstrous threat within the horror genre: Natural, Supernatural, Psychological and Scientific (2001: 9–10). The monster of *28 Days Later* – the Rage virus and, consequently, the infected – are firmly in a scientific definition, for they are the product of experimentation that has unintentionally contaminated society. Released post 9/11, the fear that the Rage virus and the infected induce within the viewer can be associated with their awareness of genetic tampering, terrorist attacks and the devastating potential of viral weaponry[1]. Given this, the threat of *28 Days Later* can be seen to be echoing the concerns and anxieties of contemporary British culture.

INFLUENCES

It might be argued that Garland's script is a series of references and homages to, or, perhaps more precisely, a contemporary reworking of *The Day of the Triffids*. Either way, *28 Days Later* clearly functions in an extreme postmodernist manner with the film referencing or borrowing from other written and visual texts[2]. When asked in an interview about the origins of the film, Garland responded:

> '…I got the idea from other people like [John] Wyndham who wrote this book *The Day of the Triffids* and J. G. Ballard. I am a big fan of J. G. Ballard, British science fiction… and also post-apocalyptic films… I suppose I'm really thinking of things like *Dawn of the Dead (George A. Romero, 1978)* and *Night of the Living Dead (George A. Romero, 1968)* and *Omega Man (Boris Sagal, 1971), stuff like that…'* (Lee, 2006)

Of all these influences, Garland's script bears the strongest resemblance to Wyndham's *Triffids*: both male protagonists – Bill in *Triffids* and Jim in *28 Days Later* – wake up to find themselves in a Britain completely changed by a singular destructive event. Upon investigating the cause and impact of the incident they meet – and fall in love with – a young woman. As they travel through a desolate London they encounter more survivors and increasingly violent situations. In an effort to escape, both parties head out into the country but before they can escape the threat completely they encounter a potentially dangerous military force.

Because of these similarities, it is possible to argue that Wyndham's novel forms the basic narrative structure of *28 Days Later* and, as if to place further emphasis upon this, Garland introduces his protagonist, Jim, in the same manner as Wyndham: both begin their narratives incapacitated, lying in hospital recovering from a potentially severe accident. Wyndham's Bill has been stung by a Triffid, whilst Garland's Jim has being lying in a coma after a road accident. While Bill's temporary blindness has saved him from witnessing the spectacular meteor shower that has blinded the majority of the population, Jim's coma has effectively left him for dead.

Like Wyndham, Garland gives his narrative a title that refers to time, with both writers using the measurement of days to describe the timeframe of their narratives. Ben wakes up on the first day of the Triffids realising their potential dominion whilst Jim wakes up 28 days after the viral outbreak. By using the measurement of days, the appalling conditions of a suddenly collapsed society are given greater impact. For Ben, a mere day has resulted in the majority of the populace of Britain being rendered blind; 28 days of viral contagion has rendered the British population either in hiding, infected or dead. As a consequence, both titles deliberately raise the question that, if it only takes a matter of days to decimate an established society, what might happen in the weeks, the months and the years that follow?

Both narratives answer this question but with opposing solutions. Wyndham resolves his narrative with small groups of survivors trying to re-establish society while still under the threat of the Triffids. It is a bleak ending and one that is not out of place within the British post-apocalyptic tradition. Given this, Garland's conclusion is surprisingly positive as the narrative ends with the implication that the epidemic will be short lived. Both endings are sympathetic to the internal logical of their narratives, particularly *28 Days Later* where the script places great emphasis upon realism: given that the infected are still biologically human and not 'zombies', Garland concludes that, without eating, these people will die from starvation. The film ends with an image of hope – a foreign jet flies over the countryside looking for survivors as the first of the infected collapse and die.

This sense of realism permeates both works, with each examining the disastrous situation within the timeframe of their authorship. Wyndham's work emphasises the middle classes of Britain, exploring how they would cope without the defining unconscious adherence to law and order, without electricity or communication systems. In Wyndham's view the collapse of society is not necessarily predicated upon mass death; it can lie in the removal of that which is taken for granted and from the small details that define the patterns of daily life. Without these defining parameters societal collapse spreads quicker as psychological corruption parallels the corruption of society itself. Although Garland's infected Britain embraces these notions it is not specifically dwelt upon. The images of London destroyed by the Rage infected population are both aesthetic and brief, relying upon the use of deserted generic landmarks – amongst others, the Houses of Parliament, Trafalgar Square and the Cenotaph – for their impact. Having effectively dealt with the national situation, Garland and Boyle then focus on a localised sense of realism and examine the impact of the singular event upon their protagonist. It is here that Garland's script begins to establish its own identity as it allows one of the film's central themes to become evident: the family.

THE FAMILY

So strong is this theme that it is possible to interpret the entire film as a critique of the importance of the family. During the course of the narrative, Jim will interact with three different families – his biological family, Frank's family and Major West's 'family'. By the narrative's end, all of them have been destroyed by the virus. The manner in which

Fig. 1: The death of Jim's biological parents

Jim relates to these family groups is important for they act as significant points within his own development, marking out his transition from a confused and ineffectual individual to one who is strong and capable. As a consequence the narrative becomes, as Boyle states in the Region 2 DVD commentary, 'Jimmy's search for himself' (2003). This search concludes with Jim assuming the role of male protector – effectively the patriarch of the family – and enables him to defend those closest to him. Because of these positive, but also aggressive, actions, Jim earns himself not only the right to survive but also the right to his own family.

The first family group Jim encounters is his own biological family: despite Selena's protest, Jim insists that they visit his parent's home. Upon entering their house, the colour palette of the film changes, shifting from the muted grey tones of the city to the golden hues of the parental home. The connotations are obvious: the outside world is a cold and dangerous place but inside, within the private space of the family, everything is warm and safe. The tonal shift also implies a sense of nostalgia, defining the house as a repository of happy memories, yet both the characters and the audience know that Jim's parents are, more than likely, dead; because of this contrast, the scenes inside the home are even more poignant and all the more tragic.

Jim finds his parents in their bedroom (Fig. 1). Both are dead, lying on the bed, their arms around each other, and a photograph of a young Jim held between them. A spilt bottle of pills, a half empty wine bottle and a wine glass stand on the bedside table. Jim pauses, unable to react. He then reaches out and, before pulling the bed sheets over their bodies, takes the photograph from between them[3]. Boyle then cuts to a medium close-up of Jim's hands, holding the creased photograph. The warm glow has now slipped back into the steel grey tones of reality. The golden tones of nostalgia and happiness have all gone, having died with his parents' suicide. Jim turns the photograph over and reads the inscription, written in clear and deliberate letters: '*Jim – with endless love, we left you sleeping. Now we are sleeping with you. Don't wake up*'. Their death overwhelms both Jim and the audience. As he mourns their loss we realise that in such a dire situation, when everything seems lost, suicide becomes a viable, even attractive, option.

The second family unit that Jim encounters is Frank (Brendan Gleeson) and his daughter Hannah. Walking back through London, Jim looks up and – in another reference to *Day of the Triffids* – sees a set of Christmas tree lights flashing near the top of the tower block. Realising there could be more survivors, Jim and Selena head toward the flats. Entering the block they begin the long climb up the stairwell but are soon pursued by a group of infected. As they run up the stairs they encounter a large figure clad in protective black clothing, defensively holding a riot shield and truncheon. In a muffled voice, this person tells them to get behind him and get inside. They push past and enter into his apartment as the unknown man efficiently kills two of the infected.

Confused, Jim and Selena watch the man step into the hallway and lock the door. His bulk fills the doorway, the black protective clothing a stark contrast to the soft, warm orange glow of the interior lights. He almost appears as a shadow, a deep negative space within the comfort of the domestic surroundings. The man drops his riot shield and truncheon and then begins to peel away the layers of protection[4] to steadily reveal himself. He is still a big man but his extended hand, warm smile and soft Irish voice as introduces himself – 'I'm Frank' – are all in contrast to the imposing and violent figure Jim and Selena encountered on the stairwell.

Frank introduces his daughter, Hannah, and before long tells them of a military broadcast he has been erratically receiving, one that promises both protection and the answer to infection – 'Salvation is here.' After some argument, the four decide to make the journey north, to Manchester in the hope of finding this promised safe haven. The journey there is punctuated by a visit to Budgens food store (a further homage – this time to *Dawn of the Dead*), a dangerous drive through a tunnel and an equally dangerous stop at an abandoned garage.

The garage sequence is of some importance in relation to Jim's development as up until this point he has relied upon other people to either tell him what to do or to rescue him from the infected. Getting out of Frank's black cab, Jim picks up a baseball bat and, despite Selena's warnings, wanders off into the garage restaurant. Inside he finds, amongst the

Fig. 2: The death of innocence

dead, a mother and her baby. Turning away from their corpses, he shouts out 'Hello?' only to be attacked by an infected child[5]. Unable to escape, Jim batters the boy to death. Walking back out onto the forecourt, Selena asks him if he found anything. 'No,' he says, 'lets just get out of here.' As brief as this scene is, it has the potential to be read as

Jim's first steps towards finding himself. His assault on the infected boy can be read as a cathartic moment; in killing the boy to protect himself he has symbolically killed the child within himself (Fig. 2).

As the four continue their journey, they stop at a ruined abbey for a picnic. This short sequence is perhaps the most pivotal in the entire film for the dialogue and action draw together many of the film's themes and establish the emotional charge necessary for the final third of the narrative.

Laying out a blanket and spreading out large amounts of food, the four survivors indulge themselves. Amidst all the chaos and destruction of the Rage pandemic, this scene is a brief moment of calm: momentarily immune to all that has happened, the four survivors sit and eat and laugh. It is as if this was a normal family day out – the children sit and eat, talk and laugh whilst the parent stands over them, enjoying watching them enjoy themselves. The backdrop of the ruin consolidates the idea that these four people are merely out for a day in the country. Yet, as a signifier, the ruins represent the collapse of a previous social order (and so reflect the consequences of the Rage virus) as well as implying that all the beautiful sunlit architecture Jim walked through early in the film will end up in a similar state: ruins from the past portend the ruins of the future.

Whilst Jim, Selena and Hannah talk with their mouths full, Frank takes an apple and walks across the field. He stands and looks out across the green expanse and calls out to his 'children' (Fig. 3). They walk over to him, still eating. Frank gestures over to a field and cutting to their point of view the audience sees four horses running through the lush

grass. 'Like a family' says Frank. Hannah looks up at him. 'Do you think they are infected?' 'No,' replies Frank, 'they're doing just fine.' They watch the horses run back and forth until Jim says there's more food to be eaten. Laughing, the three children run back to the food leaving Frank alone. He takes a bite from his apple and then blows the horses a kiss.

Fig. 3: The surrogate family

Later, as Frank and Hannah pack away the food, Jim and Selena walk around the ruins, stopping to watch father and daughter. With her arms folded across her chest, Selena turns to Jim and says '…all the death, all the shit, it doesn't really mean anything to Frank and Hannah because, well she's got her dad and he's got his daughter. So I was wrong when I said staying alive is as good as it gets.' Selena then leans over and quickly kisses Jim on the cheek. Jim smiles and looks across to Frank. He smiles back and says, 'It's getting late. I think we'd better stay here for the night'.

Up to this point, this sequence can be read as blatantly bringing to the fore the film's underlying concept of the family. The horses function symbolically for they represent an idealised view of the functioning family running free. They are, as Frank says, 'doing just fine'. Eating together, talking, arguing and playing are steadily bringing the four characters closer together and imply for the first time, a sense of hope within the narrative – Hannah has her father and Selena's dialogue implies that she has Jim. Together, the four have each other and so form a basic family unit. Selena's dialogue functions in two ways within this context as it consolidates the idea that safety and security reside within the unity of the group as well as being the first moment in which Selena allows herself to be emotional. Her dialogue is almost confessional, an apology for not believing in anything other than survival. It subtly suggests that even in all the destruction, survival is not simply about existing but about the positive, passive reconstruction of a new social order. It will be ironic then that when the four finally arrive at the military base, the plans for a new society will be based on violence.

The abbey sequence continues with Jim and Hannah trying to sleep around a camp fire. Frank sits away from them, looking out into the darkness as if a soldier on patrol, the father acting as the prime protector whilst Selena sleeps, a machete held tightly in her hand. Hannah asks Jim if he knows how Selena fell asleep so quickly. He rolls onto his side and wakes Selena to ask her. She rummages through her coat and produces a bag of tablets. 'Valium' she says and goes back to sleep. Jim takes one and Hannah asks her father if she can have one too. He says no but Jim intervenes and suggests that Frank let his daughter live a little, and Frank acquiesces.

Jim falls asleep but slips into a nightmare induced by the Valium: he wakes up in the ruins to find that everyone has gone. Alone again, he panics and runs out into the fields, shouting for Frank and Hannah, instead of Selena. This brief moment emphasises Jim's need for a family and clearly indicates that he wants Frank as a surrogate father and Hannah as a surrogate sister. The scene concludes with Frank kneeling down by Jim and gently placing his hand on Jim's shoulder: 'Ssshhh,' he says, 'you're having a bad dream, that's all.' Jim briefly opens his eyes and says 'thanks, dad' before falling back to sleep.

This single line of dialogue is essential to the underlying theme of the family. With his biological father dead, Jim can now begin the search for himself. In order to do this he must first look for a surrogate to fill the void left by his deceased father but as he searches for that person he steadily comes to realise that if he is to survive he must become that which he is searching for – a strong and capable adult. Upon meeting Frank it is obvious that Jim has found someone he believes can take on the patriarchal role for him. As previously stated, Frank is both a kind and generous man but one who is also strong and as brutal as Selena, if the situation requires it. His willingness to risk infection (which in turn would orphan his own daughter) demonstrates his selflessness, a quality which Jim will eventually absorb and demonstrate in order to save Selena and Hannah.

The third family Jim encounters is represented by Major Henry West (Christopher Eccleston) and the remains of his platoon. Having reached the military blockade in Manchester, the four survivors find it deserted. Whilst this seems to come as no surprise to Selena or Jim, Frank is furious and storms off into the blockade. Sitting on his own, Frank becomes accidentally infected when a single drop of blood from an infected corpse falls into his eye. As he tries to wipe the blood out, Hannah appears and asks him if he is alright. Just before the virus takes hold of him, Frank manages to tell his daughter he loves her. Frank begins to convulse and then turns upon Hannah. She screams and Jim and Selena come to her aid but instead of lunging forward and killing Frank, Selena instead takes hold of Hannah and holds her close, trying to shield her eyes from the now Rage infected Frank. Jim seems momentarily lost but is suddenly galvanised into action as Selena screams at him to kill Frank. Raising his baseball bat, Jim approaches him.

It is another tragic moment for this scene plays out the loss of another father. Jim has already witnessed his own father's corpse and now he must kill Frank and, by doing so, kill the man he has chosen to be his surrogate father. Jim readies himself for the task, perhaps unconsciously acknowledging that when Frank is dead he will have to take on the role that Frank so capably filled. He raises his bat but before he can strike, Frank is shot dead by a group of soldiers.

There is a certain sense of balance in this death. Jim and Selena have both been orphaned by the virus so in terms of the narrative's underlying agenda, in order for the family unit, and a new equilibrium, to be restored everyone must be free of their biological family. Only when Frank is dead and Hannah orphaned can Jim begin to assume his role as the father and begin to form his own surrogate family.

The soldiers, protected in their contamination suits, take Jim, Selena and Hannah back to their base, a stately home that Major West has fortified against the infected hordes. West welcomes the survivors and attempts to establish a friendly relationship with Jim.

As West shows Jim around the compound it becomes apparent that the Major is intent upon re-establishing the fallen British society: 'Secondary to protection, our job is to rebuild, start again.' So intent on this 'mission' West has had Private Mailer (Marvin Campbell), one of his infected soldiers, captured and chained to a wall as an experiment[6]. West has rationalised that the infected kill not to eat but merely to slake their rage. As a consequence the need to eat has been forgotten. Logically, West assumes that the infected do not need to be killed because they will die of starvation. The experimental soldier will tell West how long it takes for an infected to die and give him an indication of how long the survivors have to wait before they can venture back out into the world.

As the tour continues a sense of family develops, with West acting as a patriarchal father whilst his soldiers form his family of sons. There is even an attempt at one of the soldiers being a mother: Private Jones (Leo Bill) stands in the kitchen wearing a pink gingham apron. 'Our resident tin opener' comments West as Jones prepares the evening meal. The mockery of Jones' role is enhanced by two other soldiers who enter the kitchen and begin to throw food at each other, as if Jones' naughty children.

This family is a perverse one for it is wholly dominated by Major West. His rank elevates him into the role of father but also assures him a position of further authority: with virtually all the populace infected or dead, Britain is left without a system of law and order. With no other members of established authority apparently alive, Major West is effectively in charge. Because of this, both his men and the three remaining survivors are subordinate to him. He sternly rules his house and punishes those who question him. This enforced control agitates Selena who believes that they are not safe in the compound. And she is right: it transpires that when West began to face mutiny within his ranks, he promised them survivors, particularly women with whom the soldiers can rape; although clearly wrong, West justifies these actions to himself by seeing them as a means of repopulating the British society. In West's view, the national 'family' will not be built upon unity, as Frank's surrogate family implied, but the bastard product of sex crimes.

Realising West's intentions for Selena and Hannah, Jim attempts to escape with the women. Captured and knocked unconscious, he is taken to the perimeter of the manor house to be executed. Escaping from his executioners, Jim regresses to a primal, almost Rage infected state and begins a one-man assault upon the manor house. Killing most of the soldiers himself, Jim finally manages to rescue Selena and Hannah but is shot in the stomach by Major West as they try and leave the house.

THE RECONSTRUCTION OF THE FAMILY UNIT

28 Days Later concludes on a positive note: in a visual echo from the opening (Fig. 4) Jim wakes up in a remote farmhouse, having recovered from the gunshot wound (Fig. 5). In another room Selena and Hannah are sewing together large sections of white fabric. Chickens wander around outside, pecking at the dirt. Having literally escaped to the countryside, the aspiration of many a family unit, it would seem that the three characters are surviving the pandemic, even prospering. With their parents dead, Jim, Selena and Hannah are unified not just through circumstance but also through loss. As orphans, they are brought together to form a surrogate family unit: Hannah as the confident daughter, Selena as the strong and independent mother and Jim as the protective father. As Garland says '…you end up with a family. You've got a mother, a father, and a daughter but none of them are actually related. They've all stopped being individuals; they've become a unit which is how they survived this thing' (Aames, 2006). Everything, at least until 28 weeks later, is now safe (see Appendix I).

Fig. 4: Jim wakes up alone

Fig. 5: Jim wakes up alone... again

ALTERNATE ENDING

One of the possible alternate endings for *28 Days Later* focused upon Jim and his need for both a father figure and family. In this version of the narrative[7], the final act involving the soldiers and their attempts to imprison and rape Selena and Hannah were completely removed and replaced with a sequence involving a search for a possible cure for the virus: with Frank infected but incapacitated, Jim and Selena take him and Hannah to the research centre that was the scene of the original outbreak. After a series of events they finally establish that the only cure is a complete blood transfusion so Jim, perhaps finally acknowledging to himself the power of the Father, willingly sacrifices himself so that Frank may be cured and that Hannah can have her father back. This version of the film ends as it began, with Jim lying alone on a hospital bed, but now Rage infected. Although this ending underlines a number of the film's themes it is implausible. The narrative establishes early on that even a single drop of Rage-infected blood is enough to contaminate, rendering a complete blood transfusion impossible. Even so, it is an ending of some interest as the intention does consolidate Jim's continued belief and commitment to the idea of the father, to such an extent that he will willingly sacrifice his own life. In some ways Jim's contamination (and presumed death) could be construed as heroic for he is able to re-establish the family unit. But in terms of the long term survival of the population his act is counter-productive – it would be better that he survive and, as he does in the film, form a basic family unit with Selena as his partner and mother of his children whilst Hannah functions as their surrogate daughter.

THE RAGE VIRUS

If the themes of the family and the search for a father are the narrative's underlying concepts, then the Rage virus is its most vivid idea. This fictional disease is a blood borne virus so, visually, it is connected to the colour red. Symbolically red is already an emotionally charged colour, with interpretations varying from love to extreme rage. Within *28 Days Later* this colour is positioned as violent: the colour of the infected's eyes, the spitting and spewing of infected blood and the bloody assaults all code the presence of this colour as dangerous. It is presumably intentionally ironic then that when Selena and Hannah are forced to dress up for the soldiers' pleasure, the dresses they are given are red in colour. Here the colour unifies both the pretence of romance and the violent rapes the soldiers intend to commit into one single image – a red dress.

Because the virus is blood borne, connections can be made between contemporary, real world diseases, particularly HIV and Ebola. Herein lies the true horror of *28 Days Later* for this metaphoric value of the virus plays upon both the audience's paranoia of infections and of their invisible absorption into the mass population. Just as HIV and Ebola collapse bodily systems, the Rage virus reduces the human state to the reflex action of violence. Because of this relationship it can also be suggested that the fear generated by the Rage virus connects to our rational need for individualism: our sense of individuality is enclosed within the private space of our minds and our bodies, with our skin acting as the fragile boundary between the public and the private, the contained self and the uncontained masses. But once that boundary is penetrated or contaminated then our individuality has the potential to be destabilised by sickness and illness. The fear of bodily collapse becomes inextricably linked to our status as an individual. As a consequence, contamination from the Rage virus represents the disintegration of the individual for, once infected, all sense of rationality and individuality are erased as the compulsive urge for intense violence dominates. As a consequence, individuality is forever lost and an infected person simply becomes part of the contaminated masses.

Although these parallels are evident within the film, when he was writing the script, Garland saw the Rage virus as another type of disease:

> '[The film] is just a paranoid story coming out of a paranoid time. Lots of stuff was happening [in Britain] that felt like the right kind of social subtext or social commentary that you could put into a science fiction film. Danny [Boyle] was particularly interested in issues that had to do with social rage – the increase of rage in our society, road rage and other things. Also our government's inabilities to deal with things like BSE, Foot and Mouth. You always felt that if a virus exploded into our country, our government would be twenty steps behind wherever the virus was.' (Newman, 2007)

This comment firmly anchors the Rage virus's metaphoric potential as a uniquely British condition. Although BSE (Bovine Spongiform Encephalopathy) is present globally, when Garland was writing *28 Days Later* the agricultural landscape of Britain was effectively being altered by an outbreak of the disease. Over a period of a few short months thousands of cattle that were either contaminated or suspected of contamination were killed, their carcasses piled into trenches and burnt. The epidemic predictably made regular headline news, with newspapers and televised news reports featuring harrowing images of burning pyres of cattle alongside the distraught farmers whose livelihood had been irreversibly affected by the outbreak. By the end of the epidemic it was estimated that 179,000 heads of cattle were infected and a total of 4.4 million killed as a precaution[8]. With such a significant number of livestock destroyed, the rural British landscape became a real world counterpart to Garland's abandoned London: instead of a city empty of people, the countryside was empty of cattle. As a consequence of this one viral outbreak, Britain was (and currently remains) the country worst affected by

Fig. 6: The British countryside welcomes you

the disease. This relationship indicates that, taken as a whole, *28 Days Later* functions as a metaphor for the times as it fictionalises national events and, in true post-apocalyptic manner, takes them to their most extreme manifestation – the annihilation of a populace (Fig. 6).

REPRESENTATION: SELENA

It is important to remember that Selena's representation needs to be interpreted within the context of the narrative: a pandemic has occurred, infecting virtually the entire British population. With thousands dead and equally thousands infected, those who have survived are existing (as opposed to living) under extreme conditions and duress. Because of this, Selena has become a hardened survivor, someone who is simply living day to day. As previously commented upon, Selena has allowed the situation to condition her to such an extent that she is emotionally shut down and has sublimated her sense of humanity to the primal urge to survive. In a way this emotional state can be paralleled with that of the infected: their sole urge is to express extreme rage whilst Selena's is to simply survive. Any notion of searching for other survivors or the consideration of the situation beyond the next day seems beyond her capabilities.

Yet for all this, from the very start Selena is depicted as a strong and independent woman. In some respects, Selena's almost primitive desire for survival can be read as an attempt at countertype. Instead of being the weak female of countless horror and science fiction films, relegated to victim or simply screaming at the threat, Selena dominates the groups she encounters with a masculine superiority. She tells Jim what to do, she argues with Frank and, perhaps more importantly, she is capable of defending herself and those within her charge.

As the narrative progresses Selena steadily shifts from an emotionally closed off masculine figure to a balanced contemporary female. Her experiences with Jim and then Frank and Hannah present other aspects of her and steadily break down the barriers she has constructed between her emotions and the current situation. Even while this occurs, Garland and Boyle never jeopardise her mode of representation. Her emotional expression allows her to communicate her feminine side yet she retains her masculine superiority and strength: whilst sleeping, one hand remains firmly around the handle of her machete, she continually argues with all the men and when confronted with her would-be rapists, she does all she can to defend herself.

Because the film occurs within a post-apocalyptic construct, it is difficult to determine whether Garland and Boyle's depiction of Selena as a contemporary British female is positive or not. From one perspective it is positive for she is capable and independent, an equal to her male counterparts. Yet, from another perspective her emotional closure presents her as repressed and unable to cope emotionally with all that has happened. Coupled with this is the fact that Selena is played by black actress, Naomi Harris. Her ethnicity brings further representational questions to the character (and draws significant parallels with Romero's *Night of the Living Dead* which also featured a strong and independent black protagonist) but, once again, perhaps these questions of representation are void due to the pandemic. In such a situation everyone is equal for everyone has the potential for infection and survival.

One means of resolving this representational conflict is to examine the film's conclusion from Todorov's perspective. As already discussed, Todorov suggests a narrative begins with normality. This normality is disrupted but by the narrative's end the conflicts have been resolved and a new normality established. As Selena passes through the stages of Todorov's theory her character is constructed. The audience has no knowledge of her character prior to the pandemic so her representation begins at Todorov's stage of disruption: with the virus in full control, Selena represses her 'feminine' emotions and maintains their suppression through adopting a 'masculine' sensibility. Once the threat has been resolved (Major West and his soldiers killed, the infected dying of starvation and a foreign fighter jet flying over the countryside), the new normality is restored. And, although the audience only see a few select moments of this new society, it is enough to, as it were, represent Selena's representation: instead of being argumentative, strong and independent, she is shown to be working in the home, sitting at a sewing machine, stitching together lengths of fabric whilst Jim lies recovering from his wound. It is a brief moment but enough to imply that, within this new social order at least, stereotypes have been re-established: Selena is now 'wife' to Jim and 'mother' to Hannah. If this is the case then the previous state of disruption is not negative but in some respects positive, for disruption causes the collapse of gender roles and allows for the countertype to emerge[9].

This reading is compounded by the conclusion of Jim's assault on Major West's manor house: in these final moments Jim becomes the archetypal horror protagonist (the white male who is able to overcome the threat with both cunning and force) and, as a consequence, Selena is reduced to the archetypal horror heroine – weak and screaming, waiting for the Hero to come and save her, which, of course, he does.

REPRESENTATION: LONDON AS ICONOGRAPHICAL LANDSCAPE

The most popular sequence from *28 Days Later* is ironically the scene with the least incident: having awoken from the coma and found the hospital empty, Jim wanders out into the early morning and finds London deserted. His lonely walk takes in the usual tourist sites (Fig. 7): across Westminster Bridge, passing the London Eye as the sun rises, down through Whitehall to the Cenotaph. He passes an overturned red bus before

Fig. 7: Abandoned London

bending down to gather great handfuls of 20 pound notes from the pavement. Even as he quickly pushes them into a plastic carrier bag, both Jim and the audience intuit that this money is now nothing more than pieces of printed paper. There are no diegetic sounds, just as there are no bodies. All that remains is the city, the dead heart of England.

Garland and Boyle's depiction of an abandoned London[10] is simultaneously one the audience recognises but a city that they have never seen before. The success of this sequence relies on this very contradiction for the landmarks are all recognisable but irreversibly transformed by the lack of a populace. London should *not* be this quiet, this empty or this still. The implication is that a city is nothing without its people; it's their presence that makes the city what it actually is. This is all compounded by the use of stereotypical 'London' imagery: the Houses of Parliament, the Cenotaph and the red bus are familiar images the world over of London. They are synonymous with this city yet here they appear unfamiliar and dislocated.

Cinematographer Anthony Dod Mantle depicts the city through a series of strong compositional devices that exaggerate the situation the protagonist has woken up to. Each shot is strongly geometric, with the edges of buildings, abandoned vehicles or road markings creating sparse and aggressive compositions which Jim has to navigate; as Jim walks deeper into the deserted city, the camera moves further and further back, higher and higher into the sky. This has the obvious effect of reducing the harsh nature of the compositions but further isolates Jim by making him smaller and smaller within the landscape and so reinforces his sense of loneliness and the city's abandonment.

The sequence concludes with Jim walking through Piccadilly Circus. Eros is surrounded by large boards, each one covered in a multitude of handwritten messages, photographs, drawings, objects and passports (Fig. 8). Jim looks at the messages, taking some of them off to read them. It is another tragic moment and is again based on real world events. Pre-9/11, an earthquake had struck China. The communications structure collapsed and many people were missing. One way to try and find relatives was to post a handwritten message on similar large scale boards. Shortly after the terrorist attack on the World Trade Center, a similar communications board was established near Ground Zero. In reality, the message boards offer survivors hope but in the fictional construct of *28 Days Later* the messages do nothing more than represent all those that have died or become infected: London has become a cold and silent mausoleum. The streets do not need to be littered with corpses because all of those messages, one layered on top of the other, are the nation's funeral pyre.

Fig. 8: The nation's funeral pyre

ENDNOTES

[1] Significant events that would have been within the national consciousness include the cloning of livestock (Dolly the Sheep, whose cloning was announced in 1997), the UK government passing legislation prohibiting reproductive cloning of humans with the Human Reproductive Act of 2001, the 11 September 2001 terrorist attacks in America as well as the US anthrax attacks in the same year.

[2] 'We borrowed, sourced, and stole from… earlier works. Our opening sequence of a man waking in a hospital bed to find that London has been destroyed is lifted from *Day of the Triffids*. A scene set in a supermarket is a reference to the plundering of the shopping mall in *Dawn of the Dead*. The chained infected – our version of the Triffids, vampires or zombies – made his first appearance in *Day of the Dead*.'

(http://content.foxsearchlight.com/weekendread/node/270)

[3] The sense of horror was heightened for actor Cillian Murphy as it was the first time he had seen the bodies. As he has said in interview 'I didn't see the bodies until I actually opened the door. It was genuinely the first time I'd seen them. And also, they'd done this fantastic thing; they had created the smell in the room – the smell of decomposing bodies. So you went in there and saw that and there was this smell.'

(www.bbc.co.uk/films/2002/10/30/cillian_murphy_28_days_later_interview.shtml)

[4] As Frank takes off the protective clothing, the non-digetic soundtrack fades down as the digetic sound fades up: the tension filled soundtrack is replaced with *Frosty the Snowman* playing on the living room stereo. This jovial song is at odds with the previous violent sequence but adds to Frank's warm and safe demeanour.

[5] This scene can also be read as another reference to *Dawn of the Dead* as when the group of protagonists stop to refuel in this film, one of them is attacked by two undead children. It is also worth noting that the moment before Jim kills the child that a single piece of dialogue plays over the image: a child's voice saying 'I hate you.' Watching this scene closely, the infected child does not appear to say this. Because of this, one could interpret the voice as Jim's conscience and so consolidates the reading within this text.

[6] This infected soldier can be seen as a reference to the zombie Bub, in *Day of the Dead*: like Mailer, Bub was in the military before his death and has now been captured for use in Dr Logan's deranged experiments.

[7] This ending can be viewed, in storyboard format, on the Region 2 DVD release of *28 Days Later*.

[8] (http://en.wikipedia.org/ Bovine_spongiform_encephalopathy).

[9] It is perhaps worth noting that Garland and Boyle devised a third ending for the narrative in which Jim is mortally wounded. Dying in an abandoned hospital, Selena and Hannah leave his half naked body on a gurney and so, like the first alternate ending

maintains a sense of economic circularity with the films opening image of Jim. With Jim dead, the two women drive out of Manchester and into Cumbria where they establish themselves in the abandoned cottage. From the perspective of representation, this ending maintains Selena's masculine qualities and, to a certain extent, enforces her position as male and so becomes a surrogate father *and* mother to Hannah.

[10] This is not the first time an abandoned London has been depicted with such shocking clarity – the British film *Seven Days to Noon* (John and Roy Boulting, 1950) was noted for its imagery of an evacuated London.

REFERENCES

28 Days Later (2003). Directed by Danny Boyle [DVD], Los Angeles: 20th Century Fox Home Entertainment.

Aames, Ethan, 2006, 'Interview with Alex Garland, writer of *28 Days Later*', cinecon.com

(http://www.cinecon.com/news.php?id=0306121) [Cited 25 November 2006].

Le Blanc, Michelle and Odell, Colin, *Horror Films*, Hertfordshire: Pocket Essentials, 2001.

Lee, Patrick, 2006, 'In Alex Garland's *28 Days Later* old-school horror is all the rage', scifi. com

(http://www.scifi.com/Science Fictionw/issue323/interview.html) [Cited 25 November 2006].

Newman, Kim, 2007, 'The diseased world', film-makermagazine.com

(http://www.film-makermagazine.com/summer2003/features/diseased_world.php) [Cited 2 September 2007].

CHAPTER 8: *THE LAST HORROR MOVIE*

In September 2005, Tom Palmer, aged 20, armed himself with a six and a half inch hunting knife. He then went into an area of woodland near his home in Wokingham, Berkshire to join two of his friends, Steven Bayliss, aged 16 and Nuttawut Nadauld, aged 14. Once there Palmer attacked the two boys, nearly decapitating Bayliss and stabbing Nadauld in the chest. Palmer then calmly phoned the police. During his trial a number of facts about Palmer became apparent. He had first tried smoking cannabis when he was 14. By his 15 birthday he was smoking it everyday. His girlfriend, Ruth Cunningham, aged 17, had said that they would enjoy sex, often involving her being tied to the bed. They would then watch a film, usually a horror film or one that involved martial arts. During the questioning of Cunningham at Reading Crown Court, she commented that, in the days before the Palmer's attacks, he repeatedly watched *The Last Horror Movie*: 'It was about this guy who kills people and he keeps a video of it. [Palmer] said it was a wicked film – wicked as in cool' (Brown, 2007).

As Brown records in his article: 'Palmer told doctors that cannabis had worsened his anxiety and that he started seeing and hearing things. He would talk of hearing the voices of friends, even when there was nobody there. Palmer said he had begun to feel as if "bad people were going to do bad things" to him and started to arm himself against imagined aggressors.

'At sentencing, Mr. Justice David Bean acknowledged that Palmer was suffering from a mental disorder but not enough to establish diminished responsibility, continuing by saying that Palmer must serve a minimum of twenty years. After the verdict was read out, Palmer looked up to the public gallery and shouted out "I'm sorry. Sorry."' (Brown, 2007)

In light of the murders, UK distributor Tartan Video announced on 15 March 2007 that they would 'cease the future supply of any copies of *The Last Horror Movie* to retailers with immediate effect'. A spokesperson for Tartan said 'In light of such tragic events it is only right that Tartan ceases to profit from the sale of this film. Whether there is any link between watching violent entertainment and committing violent acts has never been proven, but we are taking these actions as a mark of respect for the families of all concerned' (*Time Out*, 2007).

The relationship between screen violence and real violence is a complex one. At times films are made which respond to and comment upon the violence that occurs in the real world, examining it and exploring it as means of trying to understand what the motivations were for such horrendous acts and depicting the effect, both in the long term and the short, of these terrible acts. At other times, violence in the real world is noisily blamed, by 'campaigners' and the tabloid press, on fabricated violence on the screen, even if actual evidence remains scarce: in Britain, *A Clockwork Orange* (Stanley Kubrick, 1971) was cited during the trial of Richard Palmer[1] and *Basic Instinct* (Paul Verhoven, 1992) was identified as being the trigger for a random murder of a sailor[2] whilst in the United States *Natural Born Killers* (Oliver Stone, 1994) and *The Matrix* (Andy and Larry Wachowski, 1999) have both being cited as the cause of murderous acts[3].

MAX

Fig. 1: Max, the suburban serial killer

This relationship between screen violence and real violence is both the central conceit and critical context of Julian Richards' *The Last Horror Movie* (2003): framed as a perverse video diary, the film chronicles the life and confessions of fictional serial killer Max Parry (Kevin Howarth). With a digital camera and a willing accomplice, Parry divides his time between employment as a wedding videographer and preying upon the British public. Having chosen his victim, he sometimes just kills them straight away, other times he captures them, tortures and then kills them, all live and in front of the camera.

The film begins in confessional mode, with Max directly addressing the audience and explaining his crimes to them (Fig. 1). As the film progresses, Max allows us, the audience, to view a number of his murders. We see Max assault a Traffic Warden with a hammer, then battering another victim to death with a meat tenderiser. As the audience watch

Max commit these crimes the film shifts from confessional video diary to a grotesque display of evidence.

As the film continues it becomes apparent that Max, although fully aware of what he is showing us, is not so much worried about the confession (in fact, he seems to be enjoying the opportunity to show others his 'work') but more that we understand why he is committing these crimes. At this point the audience expect an almost clichéd tract of dialogue in which Max will proclaim that he has been abused as a child, that both his parents and his childhood have constructed this persona he can no longer control. But this is not the case. In fact, Max calmly states he had a perfectly normal childhood and that he knows he is perfectly sane. And, to make matters worst, his reason for murdering all these people (Max confesses to killing at least 50 people) is not for any reason other than what he terms his 'project', a videotaped attempt to explore why we, as an audience and as a society, choose to pay to sit and watch such atrocities.

CONTEXT

To put this idea into context for the audience, Max has conceived of a conceptual vehicle in which to present this confessional project: he selected a film from his local video store, *The Last Horror Movie*, and recorded his confession over that tape. He has then returned the film and the now altered tape is hired out by unsuspecting customers. This creative context is an essential part of Max's project: he targets his audience through the very medium of the horror movie, quickly and effectively identifying those who choose to watch mindless and horrific violence in the comfort of their own home.

Given that Max is taking his project very seriously, he adds further context by leaving the first five minutes of *the Last Horror Movie* intact: this film's opening titles are a combination of voice over and abstract design. The voice over is a radio report which describes the escape of a serial killer and the failed attempts by the police to catch him. As the report continues, the screen is filled with blurs of white light and yellow lines, all combining to given the impression of a road illuminated by car headlights. The sequence ends with the headlights of an on-coming vehicle bleaching out the screen[4].

The white screen dissolves into an exterior shot of Starvin' Marvin's, a neon-lit roadside diner. Cutting to the interior, the diner is shown to be empty of customers. A lone waitress mops the floor, lost in her thoughts. Suddenly her mobile phone rings, making both the waitress and the audience jump. She answers the phone and talks to, what the audience assumes is her child, who has phoned her because they have been frightened by a horror movie. She finishes her conversation and looks over the diner. Everything looks clean and tidy. As the waitress puts her mop away there is sharp cracking sound, like breaking glass. Although scared, the waitress walks into the eating booths and treads on a Halloween masking. Thinking it some joke by her partner, she bends down to pick it up. As she does so, the escaped serial killer is revealed – wearing a bright orange boiler suit and wielding a large carving knife, he lunges at her and… the screen momentarily fills with static before cutting to the first image of Max. Sitting in his living room, he looks directly into the camera and addresses the viewer with his opening lines of dialogue:

> 'Hello. I realise this isn't what you were expecting. Let me explain. The film you hired from the video store, I recorded over it. But don't go switching off. You didn't actually miss very much – the characterisations were two-dimensional and the dialogue was frankly embarrassing. I think you'll find this more interesting.'

The film then cuts from Max to footage of him beating a man to death, with a brick, in a public toilet. The man screams as Max repeatedly batters him. Blood splashes against the wall. The camera and its operator watch and record the event.

The opening of *The Last Horror Movie* is a careful restaging of countless slasher films that proliferated during the Eighties and have survived through remakes and reinterpretations[5]. As a sub-genre, its origins began with John Carpenter's seminal *Halloween* (1978), a film that defined the template for all the subsequent slasher films: 'a killer, created by a traumatic past event, returns to their location, often a specific date featured in the title, to stalk and murder odious, inane teens with sporting or farming implements; a virginal "final girl" survives to vanquish the killer, although loopholes are usually left for their return should the film prove a success' (Marriott and Newman, 2006: 174). A further trope within the genre is the use of 'ironic' dialogue used by the killer moments before they commit the murder[6]. Although intended to be amusing and create a tension between the humour of the dialogue and the violent murder act, these poor one-liners do little but further degrade the innocent victims. Despite the stultifying unoriginality of the films (or perhaps precisely because of them), the slasher proved immensely popular, resulting in two significant impacts upon the horror genre: the establishment of horror icons (Leatherface, Michael Myers, Jason Voorhees, Freddy Krueger and Candyman) and the initiation of a further sub-genre, the serial killer narrative.

Whilst the slasher was a successful cinematic phenomenon of the 1980s, the serial killer narrative found prominence a decade later with the mainstream success of *The Silence of the Lambs* (Jonathan Demme, 1991) and the underground achievement of *Henry: Portrait of a Serial Killer* (John McNaughton, 1986). Although these two films are often cited as the beginning of this sub-genre, the heritage of the serial killer narratives goes back to Fritz Lang's seminal *M* (1931), which defined the sub-genre through its basis on real events and the narrative's ability to analyse not just the motivations of the insane individual but also to provide a 'convincing dissection of an entire society' (Marriott and Newman, 2006: 35). These essential reflective qualities are conceptually bound and suggest that this film-making practice is not necessarily sensationalist but more a product of the era in which these films are made.

It is here that Max Parry's intentions become evident. As he says to one of his female victims:

'I'm not going to say anything flippant or ironic to you. I know you won't understand but I'm going to explain a couple of things to you anyway. We're making a film of this. We're trying to do something that hasn't been done before. We're trying to make an intelligent movie about murder by actually doing the murders. I know that doesn't justify what I have done but it is interesting. That's the point: the problem is it looks like you can't do anything interesting unless you give people a shock and you can't give people a shock unless you do something really horrible.'

His comments to this dying woman not only suggest that Max is aware of slasher genre tropes, it also provides the audience with his serial killing manifesto, an agenda that is inextricably bound up in his first suggestion to the audience: 'I think you'll find this much more interesting.' By acknowledging the casual, intended-to-be-funny lines of dialogue cinematic that serial killers offer at the point of death, Max successfully manages to separate and elevate himself above that clichéd standard: Max takes his killings seriously[7] and tries, even in their dying moments, to get his victims to understand his intentions.

HUNTING

The Last Horror Movie is set in contemporary London. Initially, the city appears to be merely a backdrop to the film's events, but as the narrative progresses, the city and its suburban enclaves are presented as a cold architectural space in which Max lives, works and hunts. This context transforms suburbia almost into a cliché – if Max is a hunting predator then

Fig. 2: Max's hunting ground

this domestic space must be his concrete jungle (Fig. 2). In his DVD commentary, director Richards comments that such spaces are 'environments in which you are supposed to feel safe in' but as Max patrols the streets in his car, nowhere is safe; the seemingly innocent and anonymous middle class space becomes terrifying: dirty and wet, illuminated by the dull sodium orange glow of street lamps, people shifting in and out of the shadows, all the time being watched by Max.

In a further attempt to distance himself from the generic cinematic serial killer, Max chooses not to wear an identifying uniform, nor does he carry a signature weapon. Instead he wears casual clothes and changes his murder weapon to whatever is at hand, be that a hammer, jump leads, a knife or meat tenderiser. He also conducts most of his murders during the day. In broad daylight he assaults a traffic warden. Later he waits inside a house for the female occupant to return home. As she prepares her lunch he repeatedly stabs her. It would seem that Max's entire agenda is to subvert the tropes of the serial killer. But amongst all this difference is one revealing moment: whenever he kills, Max wears surgical gloves. Although he makes it clear they are there to ensure he leaves no finger prints their repeated presence visually signifies a death is about to occur and, as such, functions as Max's, and the film's, one concession to the serial killer stereotype.

REALISM

The impact of Richards' film depends upon the audience's acceptance of realism: the viewer has hired out the film *The Last Horror Movie*, that Max's intervention into that film is real and that the subsequent events Max chooses to show the audience are also real. In order to construct this sense of realism, Richards chose to shoot the film on digital video and with a hand-held camera. This strategy is implicit in the conceptual values of the film itself: the mode of representation has to reflect the concerns of the film; therefore it is logical that Max be a videographer (and therefore know how to use the equipment), he will need to have an accomplice in order to film him commit his murderous acts and that, due to the nature of these acts, the camera would be predominately hand-held in order to record the moment 'live'.

By presenting Max's story through the medium of a video diary, Richards aligns his film with the contemporary phenomenon of reality TV. Instead of watching the lives of others play themselves out in the confines of a house or watching celebrities try and survive a week in the jungle, Richards presents the ultimate reality show – this is murder, as and when it happens. This context exploits the film's voyeuristic properties and revels in the very fact that we, the audience, are *choosing* to watch such ugly incidents.

The idea of Max showing us his video diary also aligns *The Last Horror Movie* with the British Social Realist movement. This is evident through a range of budget, production and stylistic factors: the locations used within the film are all 'real' (as opposed to constructed sets); the footage, although edited, is often presented in long, continuous takes with the camera assuming the role of detached observer; there isn't a non-diegetic soundtrack and, contextually, the film focuses on everyday events (for Max at least). These attributes all align the film with a national realist tradition sufficiently to suggest that the film may be a perverse kind of documentary. Although Max has acknowledged to the audience that he has edited the footage he also stresses that he has taken very little out and has chosen to show his life and his 'work' as it happens, there and then and in real time.

These visual qualities, coupled with the introduction Max offers at the start of the film, strongly suggest that *The Last Horror Movie* is not so much preoccupied with serial killings but more with its observation, with the very idea that we, as an audience are complicit in the murderous act for we have chosen to watch them. In this respect, the film's prime preoccupation is the relationship between voyeur and violator. Both concepts are bound up in the notion that we, as the viewer or as part of a larger audience, actively want to watch trauma inflicted upon people and their bodies. This relationship between the viewer and the screen is a prime trait of the slasher sub-genre to the extent that it informs the film-making process (specific types of shot and image are recurrent throughout slasher films: the camera moving through the claustrophobic space as the killer chases / hunts their victim, the point-of-view from the serial killer as they approach their victim, the hand and weapon entering into the frame, the medium close-up of the inflicted injuries) as much as it informs critical readings.

Le Blanc and Odell comment upon these symbiotic elements: in relation to voyeurism, they suggest that 'the privileged viewer can watch the acts of terror detached from the proceedings. The enjoyment lies in the spectacle… linked with voyeurism is a scopophilic urge relating to the events and a helplessness that derives from being outside narrative intervention' (2001: 10). Whilst commenting upon the idea of violator they also suggest that the camera 'sees' as the killer sees and so making the audience complicit with their acts (2001: 11).

Through his use of hand-held camera and the confessional mode of presenting the narrative, Richards deftly merges the voyeur with the violator, forcing the audience to see the world as Max sees it. As they watch him kill the camera records, held there by the passive and seemingly emotionless assistant. Such is the extent of this realism that the passive camera becomes the audience's vision, placing them directly into the scene and so into contact with the murders that Max perpetrates. As Le Blanc and Odell comment, the audience literally become helpless, forced to watch and make a moral choice: the method is wholly related to Max's suggestion to the audience 'I think you'll find this much more interesting.'

STEREOTYPE

The idea of presenting a serial killer narrative in realistic terms is not wholly unique: in many respects the visual manifesto of Richards' film lies with McNaughton's *Henry: Portrait of a Serial Killer* and *Man Bites Dog* (Belvaux, Bonzel and Poelvoorde, 1992). Both films are low budget productions that place great emphasis upon the idea that the film is a very grim representation of reality. As Marriott and Newman comment, *Henry* was 'shot on location, partly because sets were beyond its budget, and the characters' grubby, dead-end boarding rooms provide a far more convincing setting… But the film's principal virtue is its scrupulously realistic depiction of a serial killer' (2006: 198). They continue by describing moments in which Henry is depicted more sympathetically, most notably through his recounting of his traumatic childhood and how that potentially constructed this violent persona[8]. Here a reason for murder is subtly suggested and compounded by Henry's murderous acts aligning themselves with the classic serial killer profile as a predator that hunts within his own ethnic group and class. As a result of this Henry is a product of society as much as his childhood. But this seemingly 'safe' rationale contrasts sharply with the representation of Max. As already stated, Max tells the audience that he is normal, that he has had an ordinary upbringing and average childhood. He has not been abused nor is he suffering from any psychological disorder. He is simply a contemporary male exploring the act of murder. With Henry, the murderous acts are, although quite brutal and graphic, actually more palatable because the audience understands that Henry is mentally ill and needs to be caught not only for the safety of the public but also for his own psychiatric needs. Yet with Max, the modern and urbane male, there is nothing to understand. He kills simply because he can.

After he has first introduced himself, Max is compelled to explain his first murder as if it might make us, the audience, somehow feel more comfortable with his actions:

> 'It's kind of a strange story how it happened. It was about five years ago now. I was walking across Hammersmith Bridge when this guy in front of me suddenly jumped off. I jumped in after him and pulled him out. Anyway, we sort of became friends after that but it wasn't a particularly healthy kind of friendship. You see, he'd had a pretty unhappy life – I'm not going to go into details – and I don't think he was too pleased to be alive but he sort of felt he had to be grateful and I thought I ought to be his friend, even though he was pretty depressing company to be honest. It was about six months later and we were standing together on this roof. He had dragged me up here to share a few insights into the world and I was standing behind him wishing I had never heard of Hammersmith Bridge when I just thought, well a) maybe I'd made a mistake pulling him out of the river because all he ever talked about was how miserable he was and b) since I'd saved his life I sort of had a few rights over him. So, I walked right up to him and pushed him over. Of course, everyone thought it was suicide. Anyway, that's how I got started.'

Although Max is at pains to distance himself from the cliché cinematic serial killer, by discussing his first kill Max begins to fit into the archetype: most slasher and serial killer films have, at some point in the narrative, the revealing moment of the killer's history. As with Henry, these brief biographies usually involve some trauma, humiliation or disfigurement that renders the killer as 'different' and so begins the chain of events that eventually lead them into killing, primarily for revenge.

Max's initiation story, to a certain extent, inverts this trait for it is his very first victim who has suffered the traumatic childhood. Max kills him simply because, he felt, having got to know this person, they no longer wanted to live. Death was something they desired and so Max helps to fulfil that need. Inherently involved in this decision is the feeling that Max felt he had some rights over this man. Here is the first indication that Max is not as stable as he makes out. He justifies this murder through a power complex – I saved you therefore I can just as easily kill you.

After he has discussed his first kill, Max reflects on the idea of the serial killer in the real world and deconstructs his methods. He says he kills '…men, woman, I don't really care. For the first couple of months I went a bit mental and did about 20 but after that I calmed down a bit'; and then comments that in order to avoid being profiled by the police, he uses his imagination by constantly changing the location of the murder, by changing his choice of victim (and so hunting outside of his own social I/ ethnic group) and choice of murder weapon. He also states that he occasionally steals something in order to lead the police into believing the motive for the crime was robbery. But, Max concludes, '…the problem is you don't get a lot of coverage. You don't really get to make a statement and that's why I have decided to make this film.'

MOTIVATION

Whilst filming a wedding, Max hides amongst the bushes and secretly films the recently married groom kissing another woman. Max moves to try and get a better shot but in doing so reveals his presence. Unable to run away, the groom beats Max up. Having shown the audience the footage of himself been beaten, Max looks into the camera and asks if we, the audience, are wondering why he showed us that. He pauses and then holds up a newspaper. Next to a photograph of the groom is the headline 'Lives torn apart by horrific murder' (Fig. 3). Max lowers the paper and again addresses the audience: 'Wanna see what I did to him?' There is a pause, as if to give us the time to make our minds up – do we walk away, do we cover our eyes or do we sit and watch? The film then cuts to Max inside a garage, the groom tied to a chair. Max proceeds to pour petrol over his victim, who screams out for help. This annoys Max, who pauses to tell the man that 'the neighbours are over a mile away. If you wanted to be rescued you should have owned less land.' Max then pours the rest of the petrol over the groom before lighting a match. 'Are you ready?' asks Max. The film then cuts back to Max sitting in his living room. He looks intently out into the audience and repeats his question 'Are *you* ready?' Before we can decide the film cuts back to Max who throws the match onto the man; the petrol instantly ignites as the camera quickly pans across to the burning man, recording his death and his screams (Fig. 4). The camera lingers, the man thrashing about in the chair screaming before he abruptly stops, his body going limp. There is another brief pause before the film cuts back to Max. He smiles smugly at the camera: 'It couldn't have happened to a nicer guy. But that's the advantage of being a psychopath. You don't have to take any shit from people.'

Fig. 3 and 4: 'It couldn't have happened to a nicer guy'

This brief sequence is a complex one: first of all it suggests that revenge can motivate Max into murder and his comment to his victim is, ultimately, no different to the poor one-liners cinematic serial killers, such as Freddy Kruger, offer their victims, aligning Max with that which he is trying so hard to disassociate himself with. On a more revealing level, these scenes not only show Max's escalating barbarity but also demonstrate his horrifying sense of self awareness by openly stating that he is a psychopath. Here, the role of serial killer is imbued with power even over the strong. The groom, who is presented as a rich and seemingly arrogant person, is despised by Max. It is not necessarily his money that Max wants. It is more the fact that this one person not only hurts him but also hurts others by implication – on his wedding day he continues to conduct his affair with another woman.

The sequence also reinforces the film's central conceit: why do we, as paying viewers, want to watch such atrocities? Max directly engages the viewer in a dialogue between himself, his acts and the representations of those acts. He asks us if we want to see what he did and asks again if we are ready to watch the victim's immolation. He asks us not to gain answers for himself but for us, the paying audience, to question our own motivations for watching such imagery. One answer, as already implied by Max, is that we watch violent films for the purpose of entertainment. We fully accept that the film we are watching is a fabrication and that even though a character may be violently killed on screen we all unconsciously know that the actor is still alive and that they will get up, covered in fake blood, after the director has shouted 'cut'. Yet this argument does not extend to the reality of news broadcasts, where the horrifying occurs in our living rooms and those that are injured or killed do not get up after the camera has stopped recording. The question becomes not why are watching but why do we record such violent acts in the first place?

Max's opening remarks, that we may 'find this more interesting', offers an answer to this question: when confronted with the horrific we can choose to look or to turn away. Our moral compass suggests we should turn away but our compulsion dictates that we look. This conflict is most evident when a road traffic accident is encountered: we don't really want to see the trauma, yet, as horror author Stephen King has often commented, we 'rubber neck' in order to see the bloody results of the accident. It is possible that our need to look is based not on the fascination with violence but upon our desire to understand our mortality. Death is an inevitability of all life. It is unavoidable yet unpredictable. By watching death in its various forms on the news and in films, we can cathartically confront our curiosities and fears concerning death. Whilst a drama may explore death and its impact in much more emotional terms, horror films provide the audience with the opportunity to confront death on a much more visceral level and perhaps help to subconsciously exorcise some of our fears.

As the narrative progresses, it becomes apparent that this is what preoccupies Max. His 'project' and his confession are an attempt on his part to explore this fundamental fear: to witness death first hand and to question those who are dying before his camera. Although never explicitly evident, one reading of the film could be that Max is himself terrified of death. By having control over the death of his victims, Max feels that he may be able to control his own life and death. In the context of this reading, Max's first murder functions as a traumatic event: he saw someone attempt to die through choice. By saving this person, Max unconsciously called into question his own life and his own fate while simultaneously constructing a power complex that allows him to explore this question.

REALITY

As the film unfolds, Max reveals more about his personal life. The audience 'meet' his sister (Christabel Muir) and her family, his aging grandmother (Rita Davies), as well as some of his friends, including Petra (Antonia Beamish). Max explains to us that he and Petra used to be in a relationship but now they are just good friends and adding, with a smirk, 'It's lucky we're still not going out with each other – we'd probably have killed each other.' Of these subsidiary characters Petra is the one who appears the most and the one who functions most coherently in relation to the context of the film: through her appearances it becomes apparent that she is an actress who, during the course of the narrative, is offered her first lead role in a play. Her acceptance of this role coincides with the unseen assistant (Mark Stevenson) finally giving in to Max's constant urging to commit a murder himself.

Up until this point, the audience is aware of Max's assistant through implication and through brief glimpses in reflections. It would seem that Max and his colleague (who remains nameless throughout the film) have struck a deal in that he will record Max's exploits with the full intention of becoming a serial killer himself. Max goads his assistant into making his first kill, with the film cutting from their dialogue to a close-up image of Petra being strangled: there is no sound other than Petra's choking as the assistant pulls the rope tighter. Max, presumably holding the camera, does nothing to help. He simply watches, like the audience, through the lens of the camera. As Petra draws her last breath, Max slowly pulls back to a medium shot and so revealing the assistant as the killer. He looks worried, shaken by the act he has just committed. Max says 'well done' and Petra smiles as she opens her eyes and asks how good her performance was.

This playful undercurrent to the serious context of the film is evident a number of times. Here the audience is fooled into thinking that the assistant has committed his first kill yet it is revealed to be nothing more than a performance. Earlier, Max approaches a child in the street and tells him that his mummy has sent him to collect him from school. Max takes hold of the boy's hand and they walk down the street, Max pointing to his car. The scene is unbearable as the audience is led to believe that Max not only slaughters adults, he also kills children. But within one cut it is revealed that the boy is Max's nephew and his mum, Max's sister, did ask him to pick up her son. This scene is followed by a sequence in which Max visits an elderly lady. Again, the audience is led to believe that this innocent woman will become another of Max's victims but as the dialogue progresses it becomes apparent that she is Max's grandmother.

The point of these repeated misleading scenes is to prepare the audience for the film's greatest inversion. Three-quarters of the way through the film, Max again directly addresses the audience: 'You may well be wondering if this is in fact a joke. Not a very tasteful joke but a joke none the less. Well…' Max begins to laugh, 'it is… isn't it?' Max continues to laugh as the image cuts to another close-up of Petra being strangled. Again, the camera slowly pulls out as she chokes, this time revealing her to be performing the death scene onstage and in front of a live audience.

The implication is clear: all that we have so far seen has been faked. Like the violent murders in all films are staged, with rubber weapons or knives with retractable blades and lashings of fake blood, so the murders Max has presented as 'real' are also simulations. Petra dying on stage is equally as convincing as the 'deaths' the audience has witnessed Max committing. It is a good joke, well timed and well played, for the audience is granted a moment of relief. But then Max reappears, as serious as ever and politely informs us that he was joking. The murders are all real.

For the remainder of the film, we are left to wonder who is going to survive Max's random assaults. He assures us that he won't kill his family or friends, but he is not so sure about his assistant: unable to make his first kill, Max confronts his assistant with the deal that they made, questioning him about his inability to kill. At first the assistant is afraid but as the questions become more aggressive, he turns on Max with a knife. Max chooses not to show us how he resolves this situation. Instead, the film cuts from Max asking the assistant to calm down to Max, wearing a white t-shirt, his signature white gloves and a blue and white striped apron, kneeling next to his bath. From the gloves alone it is obvious that Max has killed him.

In true video diary format, Max explains to us his relationship to his assistant: he was a man who had been homeless for three years and hadn't seen his family for five years, making him untraceable should Max need to kill him. As he speaks, Max undresses the body. He then turns his attention to the body's disposal and, taking up a handsaw, Max suggests the best way to dispose of this evidence is to eat it.

In another instance of the film's playfulness, the moment when Max is about to saw the assistant's limbs off is cut to a shot of Max carrying a plate full of cooked sliced meat. He carries the steaming plate into his dining room where his sister, brother-in-law, nephews and grandma sit at the table. He places the platter down and they complement Max on his cooking skills. It is a sickening moment, watching Max serve the meat and then watching him as he watches them eat what may or may not be the cooked flesh of his assistant. The question becomes 'are they eating human flesh?' as much as 'did he kill and eat all of his other victims?'

ENDNOTES

[1] After watching *A Clockwork Orange* 'sixteen year old Richard Palmer hit a tramp over the head with two lemonade bottles until they smashed, beat him with slabs of crazy paving and when the old man staggered away battered him with two bricks and beat him with a stick. Then he left him, cycled home, and calmly went into his own home… Palmer's defence counsel, Roger Gray, said there was no evidence whatsoever that the boy was suffering from any mental disease. He was not drunk, neither had he taken drugs – what possible explanation can there be for this savagery other than the film?' (Whitehouse, 1996: 55).

[2] '*The Times* (17.8.95) carried the headline "Wife stabbed sailor after watching *Basic Instinct*", and tells how "a depressed housewife took a knife and went out looking for a stranger to stab only hours after watching the film on video"… She told the Court that the film had suggested to her that "it would be a good idea to stab a man"'. (Whitehouse, 1996: 58 –9)

[3] The case of 'Nathan Martinez, a seventeen-year-old boy charged with killing two members of his own family after watching *Natural Born Killers* ten times' (Whitehouse, 1996: 60).

> 'Josh Cooke, a nineteen-year-old in Oakton, Virginia, owned a trench coat like the one worn by Neo, the character played by Keanu Reeves in [The Matrix] and kept a poster of his hero on his bedroom wall. Then he bought a gun similar to the one used by Neo to fight evil. In February, he shot his father and mother in the basement of their home and then called the police. His lawyers say he believed he was living inside the Matrix.' (Campbell, 2003)

[4] This image of headlights rushing towards the camera is accompanied by the sound of cars colliding. In the Tartan Video DVD release of the film, director Julian Richards says in his commentary that the image and sound of the crash were symbolic of what was to come – the collision between fabricated serial killer narratives and the life story of a real serial killer.

[5] Amongst the many series, the *Friday the 13th* franchise is now up to Part 10, whilst the first is, at the time of writing, being remade. The Halloween series is now at Part 8 whilst again the original has been remade (*Halloween*, Rob Zombie, 2007). *The Texas Chainsaw Massacre* franchise has just being reinvigorated, commercially if not artistically, through remakes (*The Texas Chainsaw Massacre*, Marcus Nispel, 2005) and a prequel (*The Texas Chainsaw Massacre: The Beginning*, Jonathan Liebesman, 2006).

[6] This is usually something appallingly predictable like 'Stick around' as a victim is impaled.

[7] This is particularly evident when Max's assistant tries to kill for the first time: so incompetent is the assistant at murder that Max feels compelled to apologise to the victim before he himself slices open her throat.

[8] Marriott and Newman suggest *Henry* is loosely based on the life of serial killer, Henry Lee Lucas.

REFERENCES

Brown, David. 'Addicts conviction for murders sparks call for drug education', first published in *The Times*, 21 March 2007 (http://www.timesonline.co.uk/tol/news/uk/crime/article1545360.ece) [Accessed 25/02/08].

Campbell, Duncan. 'Matrix films blamed for series of murders by obsessed fans' (http://www.guardian.co.uk/world/2003/may/19/usa.filmnews/print) [Accessed 25/02/08].

The Last Horror Movie (2003). Directed by Julian Richards [DVD], Europe: Tartan DVD.

Le Blanc, Michelle and Odell, Colin, *Horror Films*, Hertfordshire: Pocket Essentials, 2001.

Marriott, J. and Newman, K. (eds) *Horror: The Definitive Guide to the Cinema of Fear*, London: André Deutsch Limited, 2006.

'Tartan pulls *The Last Horror Movie*', first published Time Out, 15 March 2007

(http://www.timeout.com/film/news/1771/?DCMP=OTC-RSS-Film) [Accessed 25/02/08].

Whitehouse, Mary. 'Time to face responsibility' pp. 52-61 in *Screen Violence* (ed. Karl French), London: Bloomsbury, 1996.

CHAPTER 9: *SHAUN OF THE DEAD*

Although advertised as a rom-zom-com (a romantic zombie comedy), *Shaun of the Dead* (Edgar Wright, 2004) is not the first of its kind. As co-writer Simon Pegg points out in an interview, '…strictly speaking we are not the first romantic zombie comedy because, I mean, *Brain Dead*, there was a romance in there. *Return of the Living Dead 3* is a bit of a love story'. He continues by saying that 'We wanted to take a very sort of British style of romantic comedy, in the vein of Richard Curtis and stuff and people in London, and then subvert it. In that respect, it was kind of first' (Murray, n.d.).

Shaun of the Dead is a British romcom that unfolds against the backdrop of a zombie invasion. The film begins with Shaun (Pegg) being effectively dumped by his girlfriend, Liz (Kate Ashfield) because of his apathetic attitude towards their relationship and to life in general. Persuading Liz to give him one more chance, Shaun offers to take her out for a meal the following evening but forgets to book the table. With the restaurant full, Shaun offers to take Liz to his local pub, The Winchester, instead. She refuses and their relationship is over, regardless of Shaun's attempts to patch things up. Overnight the zombie uprising begins with Shaun and his best friend, Ed (Nick Frost), waking up to two zombies in their garden. Slowly realising what has happened, Shaun and Ed set about rescuing Liz, her friends David (Dylan Moran) and Di (Lucy Davis), and Shaun's mother, Barbara (Penelope Wilton), and stepfather, Philip (Bill Nighy). After a series of events

– including the death of Philip – the group barricade themselves in The Winchester. As the evening drags on, it becomes apparent that Barbara, too, has become infected. David attempts to kill her but is confronted by Shaun, who eventually realises there is no other choice and kills her himself. As the relationships become increasingly strained, the zombie hordes break in, killing David and Di. During the last stand, Ed is bitten and left as a diversion while Shaun and Liz attempt to escape. When all seems lost, the British Army appear and save them both.

From this brief outline alone it becomes evident that *Shaun of the Dead's* comedic value – which is very much in the telling, rather than the plot – is tempered with a strong sense of melancholy. In many respects this quality is an essential part of the landscape of British comedy, where the enduring sitcoms – *Hancock's Half Hour*, *Steptoe and Son*, *Porridge*, *Rising Damp* and *Open all Hours* – have their humour tempered by the harsh and often bitter realities of life. In these series, the protagonists often have ambitions that are frustrated either by those they call family or friends or through their poor financial situation or social circumstances. The humour lies perhaps in that, regardless of absurd circumstances which the protagonists find themselves in, they continue to strive for what they want week after week.

This relationship to the sitcom is all the more prevalent in *Shaun of the Dead* for its origins stem from the cult British comedy series *Spaced* (1999–2001). Written by Pegg and Jessica Stevenson, the series concerned the lives of two twenty-something's Tim (Pegg) and Daisy (Stevenson) as they try to work out want they want from love and from life. The programme was noted for its cinematic style as much as for its humour. Director Edgar Wright adopted a highly flamboyant visual approach, with episodes often featuring rapid edited, crash-zooms and scene changes during a continuous pan. Coupled with this was Pegg and Stevenson's scripts which are littered with numerous pop culture references, particularly from horror and science fiction cinema, console games and comic books. It is from within these references that *Shaun of the Dead* emerged. Episode 3, series 1 involved Tim imagining (but more likely hallucinating from a large amount of cheap speed he had imbibed) that his reality had been taken over by the narrative of Capcom's console game *Resident Evil 2*: zombies lurch around Tim's living room, staggering towards him from all angles[1]. Armed with only a shot gun, Tim dispatches them with a bullet and a corny one-liner:

> 'We spent a morning with me [Pegg] shooting a bunch of zombies and had such a great time. We got that far and got it on TV, so we wondered what would happen if we tried to get a movie made and have it not as a fantasy but that it was really happening. That's where the kind of genesis for the film came from.' (Naugle, 2005)

From here Pegg and Wright began to the write the script, working strong comedy elements into the horrific situation of a zombie invasion while giving the story a poignant backdrop through Shaun's failing relationship with Liz. In addition, two of the essential elements of Spaced were retained – the incongruous use of the cinematic language of genre films for comedic effect and the liberal dispersal of pop culture references.

Of these references the most obvious is the film's title: *Shaun of the Dead*[2] is a play on the title of George A. Romero's seminal zombie film *Dawn of the Dead* (1979). This play on names is continued, subtly, throughout the film as each characters name rhymes with their narrative fate. So, Shaun is reborn, Liz lives, Ed ends up dead, Dave goes to the grave and his partner Di dies.

It is an absurd in-joke but it is one that defines the narrative structure of the film for the dialogue in the first half of the film covertly explains exactly what is going to happen in the second half of the film. The most blatant example of this is when Ed takes Shaun to The Winchester in an effort to console him about the breakdown of his relationship with Liz. As they sit and drink, Ed suggests a way for Shaun to forget his problems:

> *'You know what we should do tomorrow? Keep drinking. A Bloody Mary first thing, a bite at the King's Head, couple at the Little Princess, stagger back here and bang… back at the bar for shots. How's that for a slice of fried gold?'*

Once the zombie invasion begins on Sunday morning, all that Ed has planned for the day's drinking becomes manifest within the narrative, albeit not quite as he probably imagined. 'Bloody Mary' is Mary, the checkout girl from the film's title sequence who appears as the first zombie they encounter in their

Fig. 1: 'Bloody Mary'

garden (Fig. 1); the 'bite at the Kings Head' is a reference to Shaun's stepfather Philip being bitten by a zombie; the 'couple at the Little Princess' is David and Di, holed up at the flat of his ex-girlfriend ('the Little Princess'); the 'stagger back' is when Shaun and his friends impersonate zombies to get to the safety of The Winchester; and 'back at the bar for shots' references the climatic shoot-out in The Winchester.

This duality is repeated itself extensively throughout the film and is, to a great extent, nothing more than an abstract self referential joke within a film that trades partly on the viewer's appreciation of a vast range of cinematic references. So consistent, so blatant and at times so obscure are these references (such as the film being shot entirely in the widescreen ratio of 2:35 as a tribute to director John Carpenter) that the film simultaneously functions as a piece of big budget fan boy cinema and as an extraordinary piece of postmodern film-making.

HOMAGE, REFERENCE AND TRIBUTE

Wright has commented that:

> *'One of the things about the film is that it takes place completely within George Romero's universe. One of the ideas is that, if* Dawn of the Dead *is happening in Pittsburgh, this*

is what is happening in North London. In terms of, like, the rules, the folklore, we worked completely within George Romero's universe. Sort of like the idea of a parallel story.' (Murray, n.d.)

Romero's seminal *Night of the Living Dead* (1968) has often been cited as the birth of contemporary horror cinema: with grainy black and white film stock and a hand-held camera, the film subverted established traditional conventions. Character positions are undermined and the traditional protective devices against the supernatural (religion, science, love) are all rendered void as the dead are reanimated into a cannibalistic horde. Romero's film steadily became a cult classic and critically recognised, putting him into a position where a sequel, *Dawn of the Dead*, became viable. Building upon his own zombie folklore (the undead are a shambling mass, desire only to eat warm flesh and can only be killed by having their brain destroyed) and underscoring the gore with astute social comment, *Dawn* became another influential cornerstone of contemporary horror.

The success of both films lies with their appeal to different audiences: horror fans are attracted to the intense violence and increasingly explicit (and realistic) special make-up effects, while the audience of critics and academics recognised the value of Romero's social commentary. Each of the *Dead* films reconfigures the zombie as metaphor while using its female characters to make comment upon gender relations and feminist struggles.

Dawn's narrative is simple: the undead are now beginning to outnumber the living and increasingly desperate measures are been taken, resulting in two National Guardsmen, Roger and Peter, and technician Steve and his girlfriend, Fran, trying to escape the situation by stealing a helicopter. The group head towards a greenbelt shopping mall and decide to make it their new home. The correlation of the shopping mall, the surrogate family unit and the zombies all incubate Romero's commentary, with the zombies becoming the ultimate consumers roaming the mall while the men forget their situation and embrace the fraudulent comfort of material goods. Only Fran remains realistic: realising food will soon become short, she begins to grow plants and vegetables and asks to be taught to fly the helicopter. Inevitably, the situation becomes increasingly worse and concludes with the zombies breaking into the consumer haven when a band of marauder bikers deicide that they, too, want some material goods.

The impact and influence of *Dawn* can be read throughout the entirety of *Shaun of the Dead*. On a surface level there is a sustained series of background references: the

Fig. 4: Dawn of the Dead reference

film begins with a brief musical excerpt from *Dawn's* soundtrack[3] whilst the title sequence is a montage of people involved in the daily grind of work at a shopping centre, mindlessly passing products over the checkout scanner or listlessly gathering trolleys form the car park. The electrical goods shop in which Shaun works is called *Foree Electric* (Fig. 4) – a reference to the actor Ken Foree who portrays Peter in *Dawn*[4].

The opening montage suggests that the narrative's citizens are *already* zombies. Both this and subsequent scenes in the city show the public be a group of mindless, shambling workers who stagger to work, carry out their allotted tasks and then stumble back home: the opening features a group of people standing in a bus queue with each one staring into space, their skin pale and their jaws slack. This image is later repeated when Shaun gets onto the bus with these people – they all sit with blank expressions, numbed and dislocated from their surroundings. Shaun stares out of the window and witnesses a lady collapse in the street. No one goes to her aid; instead the other pedestrians just stumble past her. These images suggest a parallel reading with Romero's zombies – where as they became a metaphor for our constant consumerist cravings, Pegg and Wright's zombies make comment upon the average British worker in that they are all lost in the mindless repetition of their daily routine, their personalities, hopes and their sympathies drained into this stumbling apathy.

Shaun also borrows basic narrative structure from *Dawn* in that both films are about a set of couples coming together to form a larger group who then travel to an assumed safe haven. To begin with, this place is indeed safe but, as tempers fray and relationships become strained, the safety is compromised and the zombies begin an assault which few will survive. As a consequence, both films deal with the concept of relationships and how specific situations can be used to critique that dynamic. For Romero, his interests lay with the 'buddy' relationship between Roger and Peter and how that was paralleled with the established heterosexual relationship between Steve and Fran. For Pegg and Wright, the issue of relationships all focus upon Shaun and how he tries to (in)effectually re-establish his relationship with Liz and tries to come to terms with his mother, Barbara, marrying Philip. As Shaun struggles through these emotional experiences and the zombie uprising, he is ably, and sometimes not so ably, supported by his best friend, Ed. This relationship is a perverse parallel to Roger and Peter's. As long term friends, Shaun and Ed understand each other, sympathise with each other and, ultimately, care for each other. But in the end, it is actually this relationship that forms part of Shaun's biggest problem – his inability to grow up and assume adult responsibilities.

SHAUN

The character of Shaun is borne out of a long line of British comedy stereotypes, notably that of the Loser. As part of the British comedic tradition, the Loser is typified by an ignorance that conceals an immense lack of self confidence. They 'are the victims of their

Fig. 3: Shaun at work, not aspiring

own ambitions, failing, trying and failing again for our entertainment' (Duguid). It soon becomes apparent that their attempts to achieve these ambitions are nothing more than attempts to prove themselves within their own peer group. Predictably, these efforts can only end in failure; a humiliation that ironically often takes place in front of those peers and results in a further loss of confidence (Fig. 3). Because of this it would seem that the Loser sends out a very strong message to the audience in that their suffering suggests that we should 'accept status – don't aspire' (Duguid, 2007).

This negative reading of such characters is wholly applicable to Shaun for the first half of the narrative: the film begins with Liz trying to explain to Shaun that their relationship is going nowhere because of Shaun's unwillingness to try something new: 'Shaun, what I am trying to say is I need something more, more than spending every night in The Winchester. I want to get out there and do more interesting stuff. I want to live a little. I want you to want to do it too.' And although Shaun agrees to work at the relationship, his first attempt fails miserably and Liz breaks up with him. When he attempts to win her back with a bunch of flowers and promises, Liz reminds him that he has promised many things – to quit smoking, to go to the gym, to try and drink red wine instead of beer and to go on holiday together – but has not yet managed to keep one of them.

Up until the appearance of the zombies in his back garden, Shaun conforms to this character archetype but, as the narrative progresses, Shaun awkwardly shakes off this role and steadily takes on that of the hero as he battles his way through conflicts with his friends, his family and the zombies.

SHAUN AND THE ZOMBIES

Shaun only begins to change when the zombies directly threaten those he loves and those who have, up until now, tolerated his adolescent behaviour. Because of this, the zombies function as a perverse symbolic as they are the instigator that forces him into maturity. Without the zombie outbreak, it is probable that Shaun would have continued through his life as if he were a perpetual teenager, stumbling from one day to the next and so steadily increasing his resolve to ignore his problems.

The first evidence of his maturity is the recognition that others may need his help. Shaun immediately puts himself in charge and quickly conceives of a plan which will allow him to save those he loves. Typically, this plan is explained through a series of increasingly bizarre repetitive montages that position Shaun as a generic hero, quickly and effectively terminating the threat and rescuing the attractive women. With *Shaun of the Dead* being a comedy, things don't wholly go as planned. Regardless, Shaun ensures that he remains in charge, despite the problems he has to overcome. In a way this self-elected leadership echoes his failed attempts of leadership within the workplace: Shaun stands in front of his peer employees just before the shop opens. He clears his throat and begins by saying that 'As well as Mr. Sloman being off today, I'm afraid Ash[5] is feeling a little bit under the weather so I will be taking charge as the…' Before he can finish, Noel, the most arrogant teenager amongst them, interrupts with 'Oldest'. The others snigger as Shaun ignores the comment and continues by saying '…senior member of staff. So if we can all pull together…' Noel's phone rings. Without hesitation and despite Shaun asking him not to, Noel answers his phone. Shaun then stands with the others as Noel continues his conversation. The humiliation continues as when Noel finishes his conversation he then sends a text and addresses Shaun: 'Continue.'

Having finished his failed pep talk, Shaun corners Noel. 'Noel, phones off, it's not a social gathering' to which Noel replies, 'Yeah alright. Keep your hair on Granddad.' Noel tries to walk away but Shaun stops him – 'I'm twenty-nine, for Christ's sake! How old are you? Twenty? Twenty-one?' 'Seventeen.' And so another confrontation begins in which Shaun attempts to justify himself by saying 'I know you don't want to be here forever, I got things I wanna do with my life.' 'When?' asks Noel, but Shaun cannot answer. Noel smiles smugly as he pushes past him[6], once again taking out his phone.

Instead of facing a small group of bored, lazy, sarcastic, gum-chewing teenagers, Shaun is now confronted with a large group of shambling, groaning, flesh eating zombies. But in Shaun's mind they are equal for both groups are a threat to his very fragile sense of masculinity. This aspect of Shaun's sense of self is made comically evident in his choice of defensive weapon: instead of arming himself with an effective weapon as most males do in Zombie films (usually a shot gun), Shaun chooses a cricket bat with which to batter zombie heads. As he swings his bat back and forth, he appears as a truly British survivor making the best of a very bad situation.

The only masculine behaviour Shaun exhibits prior to the zombie outbreak is through the second-hand experience of playing console games. Although initially a signifier of Shaun's immature fantasy life, the relevance of the console game sequences become apparent as the zombies break into The Winchester. Early on in the film, Shaun's house-mate Pete (Peter Serafinowicz) confronts Shaun about Ed's laziness, his lack of hygiene and his unwillingness to provide the financial support necessary to maintain the house the three of them share. Acknowledging that Ed does need to do something to earn his keep, Shaun tries to ask Ed if he will at least clean up the flat. Wearing a crumpled t-shirt and shorts, cigarette in mouth, Ed sits on the sofa playing *Timesplitters 2*; Shaun leans over and says 'Hey, man, listen…' but then is immediately distracted by the games, '…top left… reload… nice shot!' Just like Ed's drinking plan for Sunday, this dialogue is repeated at the end of the film. Wearing his red tie around his head[7], Shaun loads the Winchester rifle as the film cuts to his point of view, recreating the point-of-view perspective of first-person shooter console games. As the zombies stagger forward, Ed repeats Shaun's dialogue '… top left… reload… nice shot!' as Shaun efficiently kills a number of the invading zombies. In this one moment, Shaun's adolescent interests save him and his friends.

Fig. 4: Liz with
Shaun, now
inspiring

Although this is a valiant effort, the film concludes with only Shaun and Liz escaping, leaving a badly injured Ed to die alone in the basement of the pub. Before leaving his best friend, Shaun crumples to the floor, sobbing: 'Man, I've really ballsed this up. I couldn't save us. I couldn't save Di or David. I couldn't even save my own mum. I'm useless.' Liz sits down next to him and says 'You shouldn't feel so responsible. You tried. You did something, that's what counts.' Finally, through Liz's validation and acceptance of him, Shaun has transgressed his role as the comedic Loser (Fig 4.).

Throughout the film the zombies have been a metaphor for Shaun's unwillingness to mature; by forcing him into taking action and being directly confronted with his problems Shaun appreciably matures. Throughout these trials Shaun steadily learns trust, faith in others, responsibility and accountability, culminating in him re-establishing his relationship with Liz but at the cost of his stepfather's, mother's and, finally, Ed's lives. The penultimate scene of the film takes place in Shaun's flat on another Sunday morning. With Pete and Ed dead, the flat is now shared by Shaun and Liz. It is clean and tidy, transformed into an adult home, a warm and safe space within which Shaun and Liz can foster their relationship. Adulthood and the security that can often bring have finally caught up with Shaun. Although this is a happy scene, there is also a certain melancholy to it: behind the sofa is a set of shelves, one of which contains only framed photographs, snapshots of Barbara and Philip, Ed and Pete, David and Di, all at happy times in their lives. It is a domestic shrine, a site of remembrance and a painful reminder of what Shaun has lost in his efforts to re-establish his relationship with Liz.

Shaun staggers into the living room and sits, like he did with Ed, next to Liz on the sofa. They discuss what they are going to do that day[8]. Liz gets up and walks into the kitchen as Shaun says that he 'might pop into the garden for a bit'. Shaun opens the garden shed and inside is Ed[9], now a zombie with a collar around his neck and a dirty *Playstation* control pad in his hands. As Shaun sits down Ed tries to bite him but is reprimanded by Shaun who then picks up his own controller and the two begin to play *Timesplitters 2* together.

Although an amusing end to the film, this scene suggests two interpretations: the first is that Shaun is no longer attached to the past and so keeps what remains of it literally safely locked away. By doing so, Shaun is now able to mature and maintain a normal, healthy relationship with Liz. Contradicting this is the suggestion that, although Shaun has grown up, he cannot quite let go of his emotional attachments to the past and so maintains that connection by keeping Ed, his childhood friend, alive and well in the garden shed. Like two naughty boys, they sit and play, just like they used to.

SHAUN AND ED

Like *An American Werewolf in London*, the narrative of *Shaun of the Dead* is based upon two relationships, one of friendship and the other romantic. Shaun, like David Kessler, connects these two groups, finding that he cannot sustain one without detriment to the other. This tension between friends and partners initiates the film's action: as Liz tries to explain to Shaun that both their lives and their relationship are going nowhere, Shaun's best friend, Ed, keeps interrupting their conversation with expletives and obnoxious comments. This is as frustrating for Liz as it is amusing for the audience. Throughout this conversation Liz criticises Ed as much as she does Shaun, pairing them both together and commenting upon them as if they were one person. This implied unity is soon made manifest when Shaun and Ed return home from the pub, drunk and playing loud music. Their house-mate Pete bursts into the room and demands they switch the music off. As they argue, Shaun manages to stutter out 'We split up with Liz today.' The following day Pete confronts Shaun about Ed not paying his share of the rent or bills. Shaun tries to defend Ed by saying that they have been friends since primary school and have effectively grown up together to which Paul coldly replies 'He's holding you back' and 'When's he going home Shaun?'

Although Shaun's quest to save Liz and his mother from the zombie hordes drives the story forward, the film comments more on the nature of friendships. Throughout the film, Shaun is repeatedly challenged by others about his relationship with Ed. Most of these comments suggest that part of Shaun's refusal to grow up is because of his relationship with Ed, with both feeding each other's childish needs and so generating a false security around their lives. And, although Shaun defends Ed, it soon becomes apparent that his friend is just as juvenile as others say he is: whilst driving to The Winchester, Ed deliberately drives fast, knocking over as many zombies as he can, he repeatedly ignores Shaun's instructions and potentially puts the group into danger. Just as society collapses around them, so does Shaun and Ed's relationship. It is worth noting that all of these tensions only occur in the exterior locations; once Shaun has managed to get everybody into The Winchester, their relationship is re-established but with a different dynamic, culminating in Ed repeatedly standing up for Shaun and physically defending him when David points the shotgun at him. In the end, it is only Ed's infection and consequent transformation into a zombie that finally allow Shaun to be free of this ultimately repressive relationship.

As Ed sits bleeding to death, he suggests to Shaun that he should make a go of it with Liz. As Shaun starts to answer him, Ed interrupts by saying 'I only hold you back.' In their final (human) moments together both friends are honest with each other. Nothing more needs to be said. Shaun smiles and puts a cigarette into Ed's mouth and lights it.

SHAUN AND PHILIP

It would appear from the films so far analysed within this book that the figure of the father looms large within contemporary British horror cinema: the strong patriarchal dominance of Lord Summerisle in *The Wicker Man* is mirrored in the overly protective mutant male of *Death Line*, whilst in *Hellraiser* the father is reduced to a weak victim, incapable of saving either himself or his family from the arcane plots of his wife and her lover. This weakness manifests itself again in *Mary Shelley's Frankenstein* and *28 Days Later* where it is passed onto the son through the death of the biological father – both Victor and Jimmy spend their respective narratives subconsciously searching for a replacement father, a strong and determined man who can take on responsibility and look after them. In the end, both sons become the image of their fathers and meet their fates as men of experience and knowledge, capable and able to take on the responsibility and violence that this brings.

Shaun neatly fits into this emerging trait as his father is already dead before the film begins. This parental figure has been replaced by a seemingly clichéd evil stepfather, Philip. From Shaun's perspective, Philip is a miserable, grumpy man who dominates his mother and suffocates her with his strict formality. Shaun, for all his naivety, simply wants his mother to be happy. But, as is typical for Shaun, he fails to realise that his mother *is* happy with Philip and all that she wants is for Shaun to accept that.

Fig. 5: Philip, the wicked step-father

Philip's first scene, in Foree Electrics, establishes his fraught relationship with Shaun. Their dialogue is no different to a father telling off his teenage son, as Philip reminds Shaun, once again, not to forget to visit his mother and to remember to bring her flowers. Shaun responds with clipped, monosyllabic answers, a stern look set on his face. The dialogue concludes with Philip saying, almost through gritted teeth, '…and don't buy some cheap posy from a garage forecourt. Right then, we look forward to seeing you on Sunday.' With that, Philip straightens his coat and marches off out of the shop as Shaun pulls a face behind his back.

Initially this friction seems to be because Philip is not Shaun's biological father, as during this scene he makes sure that everyone in the shop, including the customers, are aware of this. But, as the film progresses, it becomes apparent that the tension is more to do with that fact that Philip seems to represent to Shaun all that is negative about being an adult: dull clothes, dull job, repressed anger and anxieties, all bound up in a routine suburban life. Yet, without realising it, Shaun is already leading that life.

As Ed drives the small group recklessly towards The Winchester, Philip dies. Moments before he does, he tries to explain to Shaun his behaviour towards him:

'Being a father, it's not easy. You were 12 when I met you. You'd already grown up so much. I just wanted you to be strong and not give up because you had lost your dad... I always loved you, Shaun, and I always thought you had it in you to do well. You just needed motivation, somebody to look up to and I thought that it could be me. Just take care of your mum. There's a good boy.'

By the end of this dialogue, Shaun realises that for all that he disliked about Philip, Philip never actually disliked him, and that he was proud of any small success Shaun had achieved. Shaun's sadness comes from the realisation that he never actually gave Philip a chance because he was too preoccupied with himself to realise that he and Philip could actually have got along together. Philip's death not only marks the film's turn towards a much darker and more serious drama, but also the point at which Shaun begins to change himself to the extent that he takes on the role now left absent by his deceased stepfather, that of protector and leader.

ENDNOTES

[1] This episode was titled 'Art' and was first aired on Channel 4, 8 October 1999.

[2] The film had various titles during the writing process, including *Tea-time of the Dead* and *Dwight of the Dead*.

[3] *Figment* by S. Park.

[4] Although references to Romero and other aspects of Zombie cinema include Shaun staggering out of bed (a reference to the moist Doctor Tongue zombie at the beginning of *Day of the Dead*), the names of the restaurant and pizza delivery (Fulci's Restaurant is named after Italian horror master Lucio Fulci and Bub's Pizzas is named after Bub, the emotional aware zombie in *Day of the Dead*). David's death – by being pulled apart by zombies – is the same as Captain Rhodes death in *Day of the Dead*.

As if to add further density to these references, the background dialogue on either the television or radio makes further connections with horror cinema: one radio announcer (Mark Gatiss) comments: 'The American Deep Space Probe Omega 6 due to return to Earth this weekend unexpectedly re-entered Earth's atmosphere over England and broke apart...' which references *Night of the Living Dead* as certain characters within that film speculate that a returning space probe has brought with it some virus that reanimates the dead. In the final sequence, where Shaun and Liz sit together, the TV announcer (David Walliams) makes a reference to *28 Days Later* by saying that the idea the zombie uprising was caused by infected monkeys was 'dismissed as bull...'. Shaun then switches off the television.

[5] 'I'm afraid Ash is feeling unwell today...' is a further name reference, this time to Ash who is the protagonist of Sam Raimi's influential *Evil Dead* trilogy.

[6] Noel finally gets his comeuppance as he is seen in the closing montage as a zombie collecting shopping trolleys in a car park.

[7] The red tie around the head is a dual reference to Rambo (*First Blood* [Ted Kotcheff, 1982]) and to Christopher Walken's character Nick in *The Deer Hunter* (Michael Cimino, 1978).

[8] Another instance of previous dialogue being repeated within the film as Liz's suggestions for the day's activities mirror Ed's all day drinking plan.

[9] Yet another scene that is anticipated within the dialogue, when Pete criticises Ed by saying 'If you want to live like an animal why don't you go and live in the shed?'

REFERENCES

Duguid, Mark. 'Fools and losers' (http://www.screenonline.org.uk/tours/humour/tourBritHunour8.html) [Cited 13 July 2007].

Murray, Rebecca. 'Simon Pegg and Edgar Wright talk about *Shaun of the Dead*'

(http://movies.about.com/library/weekly/aashaun072804a.htm) [Cited 22 February 2008].

Naugle, Patrick. 'Night of the Laughing Dead: An interview with *Shaun of the Dead* Writer / Actor Simon Pegg and co-star Nick Frost', Dvdverdict.com

(http://www.dvdverdict.com/interviews/shaundead) [Cited 21 February 2008].

Shaun of the Dead (2004). Directed by Edgar Wright [DVD], Europe: Universal Pictures.

CHAPTER 10: *THE DESCENT*

Released in 2005, *The Descent* was Neil Marshall's follow-up to his acclaimed debut
Dog Soldiers (2002). Sharing similar narratives and themes to *Dog Soldiers*, *The Descent*
received positive responses from audiences and critics alike. Having directed two popular
British horror films, Marshall has begun to be identified, in some quarters, as a new hope
for this genre of British cinema. Both films are accessible and enjoyable slices of horror,
each rife with shocks and a generous amount of gore yet within their narratives lie
moments of complexity that subtly push the films towards more conceptual concerns.

SUB-GENRE: URBANOIA I

When examining the various contextual values of *The Descent* it becomes apparent that
the film coherently functions within the horror genre and the sub-genre of 'Urbanoia': a
relatively recent phenomenon, the films that constitute this body of work deal explicitly
with the conflict between the present and the past, usually enacted between rural
/ agrarian and urban / capitalist characters. The narrative trajectory of this collision
between cultures is relatively simple, beginning with the arrival of a group or family of
modern white middle class characters into the wilderness. Their reasons for entering into
the landscape are usually recreational – either for a holiday or a weekend of outdoor

pursuits. At a point relatively early in the film, the two opposing cultures will clash and this singular moment not only acts as a precursor to the unhappy events that follow but is often its instigator. As the group or family enter deeper into the unfamiliar territory of the wilderness, they are effectively hunted down and are killed one by one by their wilderness opposites, culminating in a conflict between families or social groups. As the group size diminishes it is usually the character that is perceived by the audience to be the weakest that is suddenly galvanised into violent action, steadily and efficiently hunting the hunters. An Urbanoia film usually ends with the death of the wilderness patriarch, leaving the sole survivor of modernity to stumble back to the city, bloody and traumatised.

The film to instigate this genre was most arguably *Deliverance* (1972), by British director John Boorman. Boorman and writer James Dickey reduced the plot of Dickey's source novel to its most basic of elements and used the characters' actions and reactions to the unfolding events as a means of accelerating the narrative forward. Within an all male cast, the four protagonists fulfil basic stereotypes of the then modern male. Leading the group of Atlanta businessmen is Lewis (Burt Reynolds), the calm, handsome city dweller who immerses himself in the role of survivalist during his weekend forays into the wilderness. Here he can play out his narcissistic fantasy of matching, if not besting, nature's elements. Entering into the wilderness with Lewis are Bobby, Drew and Ed, all of whom can occupy the role of the Everyman. Their plan to canoe down the Chattooga River begins well but as they enter the heart of the river they are separated.

Ed and Bobby approach the river bank and moor their canoe, deciding to take a break before they search for Lewis and Drew. As they talk, they are approached by two armed Mountain Men who rape Bobby. As the Mountain Men turn their perverse attentions to Ed, Lewis emerges out of the forest and kills the rapist.

After much argument the men hide the body and continue their journey downriver. As they pass through a gorge, a shot is fired and Drew falls into the river, dead. In the confusion, the canoes collide and the three men are thrown into the river. Managing to get themselves to the river bank, they take stock of the situation: with Drew dead, Lewis incapacitated with a badly broken leg and Bobby traumatised by his rape, it is left to Ed to assert himself in order to eliminate the threat. Taking up Lewis's bow, he hides himself amongst the rocks and waits for the second Mountain Man and kills him.

Marshall states in his *Descent* DVD commentary that the opening sequence of Sarah, Beth and Juno white-water rafting 'was a bit of a *Deliverance* reference'. He pauses and then continues by saying '... there are quite a few references throughout the film to *Deliverance*' (Marshall, 2005) (Fig. I). In some respects this may seem an understatement as Marshall's film borrows heavily from Boorman's, in terms of structure and plot

Fig. I:
Chatooga (sic)
National Park
– one of many
Deliverance
references

devices as well as through the depiction of character and their potential as stereotypes. The most obvious connection between the two films is that a single sex group have to fight for their lives whilst venturing into the wilderness. But where Boorman's film featured an all male cast, with the protagonists being hunted down by male antagonists (and so can be read as an assault on masculinity and the contemporary male), Marshall's film deviates and makes it clear that his female characters are being attacked not by other women but by specifically male monsters. Although one female Crawler does appear, she is quickly and efficiently killed, leaving a tribe of aberrant males to hunt the women. Given this difference, Marshall's film is more about the characters themselves and what they individually represent in relation to the narrative: an Urbanoia film is to deal explicitly with a Rite of Passage. The weakest group member (Sarah in *The Descent*) will have to access their repressed strength and aggression in order to successfully overcome the threat. By taking violent action the narrative implies that although two disparate communities are engaged in conflict, they are in fact no different from each other; they become interchangeable – they are us and we are them. The return to 'civilisation' of the survivor(s) marks not only the survival of the modern (or the concealed strength of the middle classes) but also a renewal of the self as a much more capable, stronger and aware individual.

It is worth while noting that the above conclusion applies only to Urbanoia films in which the survivor is male. If the survivor is female – as is the case of *The Texas Chainsaw Massacre* (Tobe Hopper, 1974), *Friday the Thirteenth* (Sean S. Cunningham, 1980) and *The Descent* – then the narrative concludes in a very different manner: although the young woman may have overcome and survived the threat, her entry back into society is marked not with a sense of renewal but to remain within their traumatic state. The final images of these narratives depict the woman, drenched in blood, screaming hysterically while she desperately clings onto some man-made object that validates her return to safety. In many ways this ending consolidates the horror genre's insistence that a normal and safe society is one that only operates in patriarchal terms. Because of this, the female survivor cannot better her male counterparts by being equally able to cope with the violent ordeal. She must instead be reduced to her passive role through the irreversible nature of trauma.

THE LANDSCAPE: EXTERIOR

An essential element of the Urbanoia film is its location: consistently a vast landscape, its narrative function is to place the protagonists within a space that initially offers them an escape from their daily experience, but will eventually isolate them from any sense of modern society in the face of mounting horror. For this reason, the landscapes of the Urbanoia genre are, predictably, expanses of desert (*The Hills Have Eyes* [Wes Craven, 1977] and *Wolf Creek* [Greg McLean, 2005]), the endless ocean (*Jaws* [Steven Spielberg, 1975]) or a dense tract of forest (*Deliverance*, *The Blair Witch Project* [Daniel Myrick and

Eduardo Sánchez, 1999], *Wrong Turn* [Rob Schmidt, 2003] and *The Descent*).These are spaces that the characters assume to be beautiful and passive, often equating them with romantic notions of escape. By assuming this, they enter into these spaces supremely confident that their contemporary bodies and equipment are all capable of handling the rigours of these landscapes. As a group of Weekend Warriors, the six women of *The Descent* fulfil certain aspects of these generic constraints.They treat the landscape as if it were a theme park, with the opening of the film depicting the three central characters taking a rollercoaster ride down white-water rapids.

As the narrative progresses their confidence in their prowess over the landscape becomes apparent in their dialogue: the women's approach to the landscape is that of a search for 'adventure'. Holly's dialogue typifies this attitude. When asked if she has explored Boreham Caverns before, she replies: 'Saw it in a book once. It's for tourists. It's not adventure. You might as well have handrails and a fucking gift shop. If you're a jumper, a caver, a climber you just do it and not give a shite.' Her experience of nature is a mixture of both first and second-hand experience, but maintains a lack of respect for the landscape.

Although the six women's motivations for entering into the wilderness function in a seemingly arrogant manner, Marshall does allow his characters a greater sense of awareness than is usually allowed for in an Urbanoia film. Their dialogue and actions throughout the film clearly indicate that these are experienced cavers: as they walk to the cave's entrance, Rebecca says that although they are only entering a Level 2 Cave System ('it's quite safe, don't worry') she still reminds the others of the potential dangers of caving. Even after the exit tunnel collapses the women know what to do and remain calm and focused, working together in an effort to find an escape route. But for all of this it is still that essential overconfidence that instigates the narrative's ordeal: Juno, the self appointed leader, leaves the cave guide book in her 4x4 as her intention is not to enter a previously discovered cave system but to find their own system and name it after Sarah. When the cave collapses her intentions are revealed and Rebecca points out 'This isn't caving. This is an ego trip.' It is Juno's overconfidence in herself and her assumed understanding of the landscape that causes the women's entrapment.

In terms of the film's visual representation, Marshall depicts the landscape as a very cold, almost dead space; each image is presented in a restrained and muted palette of cold blues, bone whites and drained greens. By continually using aerial shots of this landscape, the vast expanse of the Appalachian Mountain range is made explicit and so consolidating the women's isolation from any sense of relative safety. Marshall makes this clear in his establishing shots of Beth's car driving through the wilderness. In a reference to Stanley Kubrick's *The Shining* (1980), this aerial shot follows the path of the road until it catches up with the moving vehicle. The dull grey road appears as a thin line cutting through the dense forest; an insignificant moment of human presence within nature as the car is dwarfed by the sheer volume of the surrounding trees (Fig. 2).

This lingering ariel shot acts as a precursor to the forthcoming drama of the film. The road, with its even surface and graceful curves flanked either side by seemingly endless trees, defines the narrative's oppositions: the wilderness against the city, the primitive against the civilised, and the six women

Fig. 2: The man-made dwarfed by Nature

against the tribe of Crawlers. The road represents order within the chaos of nature and so, should anyone survive the forthcoming ordeal, will operate as the safe route back to civilisation.

THE CITY: JUNO

When watching *The Descent*, the audience may at times be unsure as to what genre it positions itself within. For the most part, the film functions as an all-girl action movie. In this context the women are all presented as masculine-feminine, an interpretation which increases as Marshall provides opportunity for the women to display their physiques and physical prowess: Juno running through the woodland in a shot that takes in – and lingers upon – her entire body; Rebecca free climbs across a chasm demonstrating extreme physical strength. As a continuum throughout the film, each of the women wear tight clothing that emphases simultaneously the muscular and sexual nature of their bodies.

Perhaps of all of the film's characters, it is potentially Juno who, in terms of gender and representation, operates in the most complex manner. The audience's sympathy for her shifts dramatically throughout the film – they know from the start that there is a tension between her and Sarah's husband Paul but her predominate function within the narrative as 'Male Hero' temporarily redeems her infidelity in the eyes of the audience. Marshall plays upon this fluctuation of sympathy twice within the film: the first is when Juno accidentally kills Beth, and the second instance is when she saves Rebecca from the Crawler. By killing Beth, it becomes possible that Sarah will never know for certain of the affair, hence her lying to Rebecca, Sam and finally to Sarah about Beth's death. In the second instance, Juno demonstrates her masculine strength by simultaneously killing one element of the narrative's threat and saving one of her party; moments after this she breaks down. Considering Juno in this manner highlights not just the shift in the audience's sympathy for her but also the very fluctuation of her character. She attempts to maintain an exterior of female strength – attractive, aware, muscular, positive and commanding – yet when these qualities are tested by a very real threat, her masculine traits falter and she demonstrates qualities that are usually aligned with weak (female) characters – crying and collapsing. It is in these moments that her guilt – for lying to the women, for foolishly leaving the map behind and for cheating on Sarah – finally surfaces.

THE WILDERNESS: CRAWLERS

The Crawlers, like all horror film monsters, carry meaning. These creatures are located within and associated with the landscape; they are part of the wilderness and embody all its primal elements in one physical body. As such they represent Nature as a primitive fear, as a violent and unpredictable force.

Given that *The Descent* is part of the Urbanoia sub-genre, the Crawlers' physical embodiment of the wilderness takes on further meanings. Within this type of film there is a conflict between two groups of people. Those characters that enter the landscape from the city represent the 'modern' whilst those people / creatures that inhabit the landscape can be seen to represent the 'wilderness'. This creates an obvious set of binary oppositions – the modern against the primitive or the present against the past. Using these terms to describe opposition generates meaningful values for the antagonistic threat and so creates for them an index of possible interpretations.

As a general observation, the threat of any Urbanoia film can be paralleled with a number of real world analogies. Some critics have interpreted the cannibalistic family of Craven's *The Hills Have Eyes* as a modern representation of Native American Indians or, given the time of its making, the Viet-Cong. What these parallels draw attention to is the guerrilla nature of the threat: these are groups of people who live in harmony with the landscape and who have a deep and explicit relationship with the wilderness. It is this knowledge that allows them to become such formidable threats, regardless of how much modern technology is sent into these primitive spaces.

By applying this notion to *The Descent*, the Crawlers function in a similar way. They are not just part of the landscape but have been conditioned by it. Their existence deep within the caves means they are virtually blind but have an acute sense of hearing. They are physically strong and dextrous, capable of climbing walls and squeezing through the tight confines of the cave tunnels. They are so in sympathy with the landscape that they are virtually part of it. Their extreme and unpredictable violence codes them as guerrilla fighters and so again draws alignments with such groups. Because of this, it is, to a certain extent, possible to suggest that a further reading of *The Descent* would be that it functions as a reaction or an interpretation of the ongoing Gulf conflict. Within this context the group of women who enter into a desolate wilderness space (the Middle East) represent the coalition forces whilst the Crawlers represent a variety of terrorist threats[2].

THE MODERN PRIMITIVE: SARAH

As the film's protagonist, Sarah embodies a range of representations and critical ideas, all of which are grounded in her status as a woman and as a mother. As the narrative progresses, Sarah will: lose her husband and daughter in a tragic accident; be trapped inside an unexplored cave system; mercy-kill her best friend; fight off a horde of primitive creatures; and discover that her other close friend was involved in an affair with her husband. As these threats to Sarah's life and sanity escalate, so too does the increasing complexity of her representation.

Within the context of both horror and Urbanoia, Sarah's position as traumatised female identifies her as the ideal character to undergo the most significant of all transitions. By surviving the accident and then witnessing further deaths, Sarah is forced to engage with situations that are seemingly out of the realms of her ability and understanding. From a positive perspective, her movement through the narrative has the potential to be a Rite of Passage where by overcoming both the obstacles of the Crawlers and confronting Juno with evidence of the affair, she can emerge from the cave exorcised of her guilt and repressions. Yet Sarah is not allowed such a positive catharsis and is instead exiled to the darkness of the cave – her Rite of Passage is not one of release but one of entering a new physical and psychological state, one which finally makes her function as the modern primitive.

The first instance of Sarah's transformation into a primitive is to create fire: she takes Holly's climbing axe and cuts a strip of material from her trousers. She then douses this in liquid paraffin from a miner's lamp she finds amongst the bones surrounding her corpse and ignites the soaked fabric (Fig. 3).

Fig. 3: Sarah and Juno, modern primatives

Making fire is the most basic of primitive of acts, with its creation offering light, warmth and heat to cook with as well as psychological security. Sarah's torch functions in the opposite manner; instead of offering warmth and safety it illuminates the horrors of the physical space, revealing the squalor of blood, bone and putrefying flesh in which the Crawlers live.

Having made fire, Sarah almost immediately engages in unarmed combat with a family of Crawlers: after Sarah has carried out her mercy killing of Beth, she is assaulted from behind by a child Crawler. With deft skill, Sarah throws the creature onto the floor and breaks its neck by repeatedly stamping on its throat. As she takes up her torch and walks away a female Crawler (her breasts are obvious even in the darkness of the cave) approaches the child's body and sniffs it. Realising it is dead, it screams and chases Sarah.

While running away, Sarah stumbles into a pit of blood and flesh, throwing the torch onto the opposite side as she falls. Emerging from the pool she is attacked by the Crawler mother. They fight and Sarah overcomes the creature by plunging a deer horn into its eye. As she lets the body go, she turns to see the Crawler father appear. Lying on the blood-wet rocks, she allows the creature to climb over her and then, slowly, she takes up an animal bone and repeatedly batters the Crawler father's skull. The sequence ends with Sarah standing in the blood red cave, torch in one hand and bone-club in the other, screaming.

This short sequence provides a significant point within the narrative, operating on three different levels. First, it is the moment of Sarah's total 'descent' into primitivism; secondly, it is a cathartic moment in which the death of Sarah's family is played out again but this time with Sarah as the aggressive instigator; and, finally, as a sequence which constructs Sarah as the horrific-feminine. Her descent into primitivism is amplified at the start of the sequence when Sarah fights the Crawler mother with her bare hands, steadily being stripped of her outer clothes and the climbing equipment from around her waist. This removal of modern materials and equipment imitates a 'stripping' back to the primitive state, one which is compounded by Sarah defending herself with her own strength and her use of a bone as a weapon.

BIRTH

Sarah's response to the Crawlers and the deaths is one that culminates in a perversely positive representation of the modern female. Instead of acting out a stereotyped female reaction to events – to collapse, to run and hide or to simply give herself up to the narrative threat – Sarah emerges as a transgressed housewife, one who takes strength from the narrative events and empowers herself and so becomes that which the others fear the most. Her transition from an apprehensive and potentially weak character is marked through a series of scenes which draw together Sarah's reactions to events with the film's *mise-en-scène*. By repeatedly placing emphasis on this parallel, Marshall plays out a series of 'birth' scenes for Sarah, with each re-birth becoming bloodier and more violent than the previous one.

Sarah's first birth takes place early on in the group's exploration of Boreham Caverns. Having taken a short break, the women look for the entrance to the next part of the system. Although Sarah finds it, the other women go first leaving Sarah to bring the kit through. Following Beth, she enters the tight tunnel and begins to crawl forward but finds she is stuck. As she tries to twist herself free she panics and starts to scream. Beth manages to turn around and calm her down. Working together, they begin to ease their way out of the tunnel but Sarah's attempts to crawl out cause the roof to collapse. Beth drags herself out of the tunnel and turns to pull Sarah out, just in time.

Given the tight confines of the tunnel and Sarah's almost foetal poses as she squeezes herself through, the *mise-en-scène* of this sequence bares similarities to a birth canal. For this first birth scene the analogy is subtle, with the emphasis being placed upon the tight confines of the tunnel and the struggle for escape. But Marshall builds upon this scene in the later births, again using the *mise-en-scène* as a clear means of equivalence. In order to ensure the audience considers this possibility, when Sarah is dragged, head first, out of the tunnel, Marshall inserts the intra-digetic sound of Sarah taking her first gasp of air when she wakes up after the accident. The sound is analogous to the child's first breath and so consolidates the notion of birth.

Sarah's second birth takes place during her slaying of the Crawler family. Sarah's emergence from the bloody pool is clearly a birthing image, one that is consolidated by the presence of the aggressive Crawler mother: emerging head first, Sarah reaches out to pull herself out of the vagina-shaped pool, gasping for air as she does so (Fig. 4). The birth serves as the transition of Sarah into the modern primitive, with her scream that concludes this sequence functioning again as if this is a child's first breath.

Fig. 4: Sarah's second birth

Interestingly this scream, as it echoes throughout the chambers of the cave, is heard by Juno, Rebecca and Sam who misinterpret it as a Crawler's scream. And so, for the audience at least, Sarah's transition into the modern primitive is made all the more complete: stripped of her comfortable, body concealing fleece and technological apparel of torch and climbing equipment, Sarah emerges out of the Crawlers bloody lair, her toned and muscular body drenched in blood and clearly on display, a bloody bone-weapon in one hand while the other holds aloft fire.

Although this scene is clearly an empowering one for Sarah within the narrative, her emergence from the lair as masculine-feminine can in some ways be interpreted as 'a masculine fantasy in which the feminine is constituted as horrific' (Stamp Lindsey, 1996: 281). Sarah's sexuality is rendered obsolete by her muscular body, by the blood that is literally soaking into her skin and by her intensely violent acts, all implying a crossing of gender boundaries. From the point of her 'birth' from the lair to her violent incapacitation of Juno, Sarah increasingly assumes the masculine / heroic role typically occupied by the (white) male. Her transition can therefore be interpreted not as an empowering change but as one that becomes 'horrific' for it upsets the established status quo of the genre – the male must vanquish the supernatural threat and save the females. It should not be the other way around.

As if responding to such a reading, Marshall initially allows a return to the genre's status quo by allowing Sarah to survive the ordeal and escape back into reality: having left Juno to die, Sarah runs through the warren of tunnels and finds an exit. Clambering up an incline of human and animal bones,

Fig. 5: Sarah's third birth

she reaches daylight. Cutting to a reverse exterior shot of the base of a tree, Marshall presents his third and final birth for Sarah. First, her hand breaks through the damp undergrowth, then her other hand appears. Reaching out and pressing down, a bloody Sarah pulls herself out from between the trees roots – an almost symbolical crotch – takes in her first lung full of fresh air and lets it out as a painful scream (Fig. 5).

THE FINAL GIRL

In her seminal text *Men, Women and Chainsaws* (1992), Carol J. Clover critically assessed horror films (and in particular the 'slasher' sub-genre) in terms of their impact upon gender. Although Clover identified certain misogynistic consistencies – women were often victims of both the narrative threat and of a patriarchal society – this was only up to a certain point within slasher films. She identified the fact that it was usually a female teenager or woman who finally defeats the narrative threat. Clover termed this character the Final Girl and defined her as the narrative's sole survivor who is uninterested in sex (and so is a virgin), resourceful and capable of taking defensive actions. As a consequence of this, Laurie in John Carpenter's *Halloween* (1978), Sally in *The Texas Chainsaw Massacre* and Alice in *Friday the 13th* all became the first Final Girls.

In narrative terms, *The Descent* can be equated to the slasher genre in that the six women are all being hunted in an enclosed space, with each one systematically being killed as the narrative draws to a close. In this respect one assumes that Beth will become the Final Girl for she is the least likely to survive yet will find her strength and overcome the threat. Yet it is Sarah who survives, bursting out into the wilderness. Given this, Sarah almost fulfils Clover's criteria for Final Girl status as she is both resourceful (her descent into primitivism) and capable of taking defensive actions (by killing numerous Crawlers and assaulting Juno) but her role as mother isolates her from the totality of this role. To a certain extent it is pedantic to state that Sarah is not completely a Final Girl purely because she does not fulfil a set criterion. But her status as Final Girl can also be questioned because of her transition into the Modern Primitive. As will be seen, Sarah's change of states actually makes her the monster and so negates her position as survivor. And, to add further complexity, Sarah does not definitely survive the ordeal for, at the film's end, she remains trapped within Boreham Caverns. It is traditional that the Final Girl terminates the narrative threat and begins the journey back to civilisation, bloody and traumatised. This does occur for Sarah – the audience sees her 'birthing' back into the wilderness and staggering to the safety of the road – yet it is undermined by her waking up once more in the cave, seemingly trapped until her death in Boreham Caverns.

THE MONSTROUS-FEMININE

The critical concept of the abject was initially explored in Julia Kristeva's seminal text *Powers of Horror* (1982) and later utilised and expanded upon by Barbara Creed in her equally seminal text *The Monstrous Feminine* (1993). Creed's exploration of abjection focuses specifically upon the then contemporary horror film (amongst others the previously discussed *Alien*, *The Exorcist* [William Friedkin, 1973] and *Carrie* [Brian De Palma, 1976]), exploring their horrific imagery in order to demonstrate that most, if not all, horror films function as terrifying because of their distinct emphasis upon the imagery of abjection. For Creed this has clear ramifications in relation to the roles and representations of female characters and the idea that they are in fact the monster, hence the term 'monstrous-feminine'. These two critical ideas have a value in the critical assessment of *The Descent* for the character of Sarah simultaneously embodies (or at least implies) both parts of these notions.

In terms of a simple definition, to 'abject' something is to reject it and to be in an abjected condition is to be in a state of rejection. In relation to horror cinema, Creed states that these notions of rejection can take place in three interrelated ways: the first is through the pure image of the abject, be that in the depiction of spilt blood, the release of vomit, salvia, and / or sweat and the lingering imagery of putrefying flesh – all of which *The Descent* has in abundance.

The second relationship is through the crossing of a border, with Creed stating 'the concept of a border is central to the construction of the monstrous in the horror film; that which crosses or threatens the "border" is abject' (2000: 66). The border exists between normal society and the abnormal society, or in more simplistic terms, the defining border between the protagonist and the antagonist, between hero and monster. Once a member of society or a member of the hero's group becomes a monster (for example through infection as in a vampire narrative) then they become at one with the monster and so become abject. It is here and in the third means of representation – the horror film's preoccupation with the maternal figure – that the character of Sarah is fully grounded into the state of abjection: as both a mother and as a character that undergoes a dramatic psychological change, Sarah finally represents the notion of abjection. By the end of the narrative she is drenched in the blood of her friends and enemies alike; she is barley able to speak; has regressed into a violent primitive state and, as the film's final images imply, has regressed into a delusional fantasy in which she can safely co-exist with her dead daughter.

Given this character's narrative trajectory, it is obvious that she embodies all three of these defining qualities of abjection. Throughout the duration of the film, Sarah (quite literally at some points) wallows in the imagery of abjection: her 'birth' emergence from the pool of blood and putrefying flesh stains her for the remainder of the film with abjection. The primary stages of her descent into primitivism see her foraging amongst putrefying flesh, whilst her increasingly violent acts towards the Crawlers spill excessive amounts of blood. Her abjection is made complete by her dreamt escape from the cave which concludes with her vomiting. Taking into account the scale of Sarah's abjection, these incidents and images (which are all powerful in their own right) can be interpreted as functioning merely as surface indications, as visual signifiers of her increasingly abject state – it is more the roles that Sarah assumes and descends into which consolidate her abjection.

As previously discussed, Sarah's narrative is focused specifically on empowering her, with the empowerment not coming through the exploration of a new cave system as Juno intended but through the descent into a state of sheer primitivism. Although this state carries the connotations previously discussed, it also carries with it the descent into abjection. Sarah's primitive state indicates that she has willingly crossed the border that lies between the modern and the primitive, the border between human and non-human. By crossing from one side to the other, from one state to another, Sarah embraces her own creeping insanity by accepting the state of abjection.

Creed interprets the crossing of the border into the abject as a vehicle by which the 'encounter between the symbolic order and that which threatens its stability' (ibid.) can take place. This encounter is given its predominate form in the sustained assault upon the six women by the Crawlers: by their very position as the 'Monster' within *The Descent's* narrative the Crawlers are automatically deemed abject – they're cannibalistic and wallow in putrefying flesh and blood, they expel gouts of saliva, they are physically different in their evolution and in respect of maternal figures there is an implied incest, for the Crawlers live in a self-contained society within the depths of Boreham Caverns. In essence, they are, like Sarah, the physical embodiment of abjection.

In becoming almost one of these creatures (primitive, aggressive, and in her final fight with the Crawlers, cannibalistic) Sarah's abjection is almost complete and so she too must now encounter the symbolic order as Creed's unstable element. As the sole survivors, Sarah and Juno attempt to escape but are eventually surrounded by a pack of Crawlers. Seemingly standing together, they successfully fight off the first assault by the Crawlers but, in the brief pause between attacks, Sarah's abjection comes to the fore as she confronts Juno with knowledge of the illicit affair. In this brief but brutal scene, Juno (with her metal pick axe, rubber wet suit and neon torch) represents all that remains of modern normality whilst Sarah, stripped of her modern accoutrements and consumed with primitive rage, is clearly its threat, and one that acts with a silent, ferocious efficiency. Instead of killing her herself, Sarah chooses to cruelly incapacitate Juno and leave her, defenceless, to be killed by the Crawlers.

Creed's third and final criterion for defining abjection within horror cinema is 'the construction of the maternal figure as abject' (2000: 67). Creed states that Kristeva 'sees the mother-child relationship as one marked by conflict: the child struggles to break free but the mother is reluctant to release it' and that 'in the child's struggle to break away, the mother becomes "abject"' (ibid.). This concept is most blatantly manifested in Sarah as she refuses to accept that her daughter, Jessie, is dead. Unable to cope with this loss, Sarah experiences increasingly realistic visions of her daughter, visions which, by the narrative's end, become her reality. This descent into a fractured psychosis becomes the true narrative drive of the film and, if taken in its entirety, is covertly a lengthy illustration of the abjected state of the maternal figure. The irony of the narrative is that the child has broken free of its mother through her tragic death yet even in death the child is still unable to free itself of her mother's grip.

It is interesting to note that in Sarah's fantasy, the father is completely absent. She has taken on both roles, functioning as an adult who can both nurture and hunt, one who can protect the clean human child and can efficiently kill the dirty non-human adults. Her transition from modern mother to primitive mother is made complete by the simultaneous embracement of her insane fantasy and her increasing state of abjection.

THE LANDSCAPE: INTERIOR

The concept of abjection can also be applied to the *mise-en-scène* of the cave system. If abjection deals with the rejection of bodily fluids and flesh, then the caves are a repository of abjection for their ground is littered with these unwanted organic materials. This sense of abjection is amplified by the presence of the women, whose flares and torch illuminate the empty chambers with a deep red light, transforming the wet, slimy space into a vacant, diseased womb, slick with fetid blood. By extending this analogy; if the caves are empty wombs, then the dark claustrophobic tunnels which the women pull themselves through operate as vaginal canals, with each tunnel leading into those womb-like spaces. As if to anticipate this relationship between cave and female reproductive organs, Juno's response to Sam's question on how to get out of the caves is 'there's only one way out of here and that's down the pipe'.

By accepting this analysis, the cave itself becomes a feminine space, one that is a bodily warren of chambers, wombs and vaginal canals. Its organic nature is activated by the mutilated flesh of those murdered and consumed by the Crawlers and emphasised by Juno's burning red flares and Sarah's torch. In presenting the cave in this manner *The Descent* offers its audiences a cold and unpleasant perspective on the nature of reproduction. Characters force themselves through tight, restricting tunnels only to emerge into dark, bloody womb-like caves. Within the recesses of these spaces albino creatures scurry around the dirty walls and floors, attacking anything other than their own kind. In the context of this analysis, the Crawlers appear like deformed foetus, the unpleasant offspring of the caverns.

The notion of birth culminates in Sarah's third and final birth out of the cave: as Juno stated earlier in the film the only way out was through the pipe so Marshall forces Sarah out of the cave through a narrow tunnel filled with bones, lingering on her struggle up towards the vagina-like opening from which she will birth herself. As a child of the cave she is perversely adult yet regressed mentally – virtually mute from the terror of the birthing process, she stumbles through the landscape screaming, clinging onto whatever she can in an effort to stabilise herself.

ENDNOTES

[1] The term 'Urbanoia' is taken from *Horror: The Definitive Guide to the Cinema of Fear* by James Marriott and Kim Newman. They describe the sub-genre as:

> 'Travel from town to country has always involved danger, as evident in the travel narratives from the myths and fairy tales underpinning Western culture to accounts of *banditti* waylaying adventurers on the Grand Tour, and it is significant that the protagonists in Urbanoia films tend to be tourists, displaying the flagrantly non-essential use of income in deprived areas that marks them as potential if not justified victims.' (2006, p.148)

[2] It is worth noting that *The Descent* itself became embroiled in a terrorist bombing: the Number 30 bus destroyed in a suicide bombing in Tavistock Square, London on 5 July 2007 bore the film's promotional poster. Although badly damaged by the explosion, the image of a bloody and battered Shauna MacDonald remained intact as did the publicity quote 'Outright terror… Bold and Brilliant'. The poster's remains acted as a surreal commentary on the events of the day.

REFERENCES

Creed, B. 'Kristeva, femininity, abjection' pp. 64-70 in *The Horror Film Reader* (ed. Kenneth Gelder), London: Routledge, 2000.

The Descent (2005). Directed by Neil Marshall [DVD], Europe: Pathe.

Lindsey, S.S. 'Horror, femininity, and Carrie's monstrous puberty' pp. 279-95 in *The Dread of Difference: Gender and the Horror Film* (ed. Barry Keith Grant), Austin: University of Texas Press, 1996.

Marriott, J. and Newman, K. (eds) *Horror: The Definitive Guide to the Cinema of Fear*, London: André Deutsch Limited, 2006.

APPENDIX I: *28 WEEKS LATER*

Whereas *28 Days Later* positioned the father as a positive figure within the family unit, the sequel, *28 Weeks Later* (Juan Carlos Fresnadillo, 2007), reconfigures the role of the father into a wholly negative force. The prologue introduces the audience to this man, Don Harris (Robert Carlyle), who during an attack by the infected abandons his wife, Alice (Catherine McCormack), in order to ensure his own safety. Somehow Don manages to survive the pandemic and becomes part of the work force that is attempting to rebuild Britain. In his role as caretaker, Don is responsible for the care and maintenance of the high-rise buildings on the Isle of Dogs, named District I by the occupying US Forces that have been commandeered for the returning populace. Amongst the first to return are his two children, teenager Tammy (Imogen Poots) and his young son Andy (Mackintosh Muggleton). Whilst settling into their new home, Tammy asks her father about the death of their mother and, instead of confessing to his cowardice, Don lies and tells his children there was nothing he could do to save her. His initial cowardice and now his lying position Don as an unreliable figure within the narrative. The re-establishment of the family unit becomes immediately unstable for it is based on the lies of the father and his inability to deal with his past actions. It is upon these essential traits that the narrative pivots for Don's past is visited upon him when his wife is discovered alive.

Although Alice only appears relatively briefly within the film, her scenes resonate with Gothic potential: she is found by her son in the abandoned family home where she has hidden herself in the attic. This room is rank with squalor. Bowls of rotting food, writhing with maggots, stand amongst the clutter on a central table, upturned chairs and other pieces of furniture lie in a tangled mass near the door. The stained curtains are drawn and cast a pale yellow glow that recalls the lighting in Jim's parents' bedroom in *28 Days Later*. The walls are covered in handwritten scrawl and masses of X's. As Andy searches the room, Alice crawls out the shadows, bitten and bloody, her hair wild and one eye stained with infection. She is, quite literally, a mad woman in the attic. Her discovery is effectively a return from the dead, a literal ghost who haunts the ancestral home. Her arrival at District I reinforces this idea, particularly in relation to Don for Alice physically becomes an element of the past manifesting itself within present, bringing with it the horror of infection.

When Don finally gets to see Alice he tries to justify his actions and asks for her forgiveness. Alice says 'I love you Don.' And they kiss. In that instant Alice's revenge is wrought as she infects her husband. Thrashing wildly as the virus takes hold Don turns on Alice and repeatedly punches her face, blood and spittle dripping from his mouth as he forces his thumbs into her eyes. For all its horrific violence, this scene carries metaphoric value: the kiss that contaminates once again aligns the Rage virus with sexual connotations, literally transforming it into a kiss of death. The scene also suggests that the virus perversely allows for Don to violently manifest his repressed guilt over his cowardice and his lying. To his mind Alice died in the cottage and killing her now is no different to leaving her to die back then.

Without parents and the infected decimating the repatriated populace, Tammy and Andy are protected by Sergeant Doyle (Jeremy Renner), a Special Forces sniper, and Chief Medial Officer Major Scarlet Ross (Rose Byrne). As the four try to escape District 1, it becomes apparent that Doyle is attracted to Scarlet and that she too may be attracted to him. With this and their mutual commitment to saving the children they form a surrogate family. Although it is one dominated by the military it is one in which the parent figures are equal: Doyle is an obvious representation of the ideal and strong patriarch whilst Scarlet herself is represented as an equally strong and ideal matriarch. With this family unit in place, it would seem that the remainder of the narrative will involve their eventual escape but, in typically bleak British apocalyptic fashion, Doyle is burnt alive whilst Scarlet is killed by Don, leaving the children once again to defend themselves. Armed with Doyle's rifle, they try to continue their escape but are confronted by their infected father. Without hesitation Tammy repeatedly shoots him.

Don's death at the hands of his daughter suggests an almost Freudian reading in which the idea of penis envy is lived out to its most extreme possibility: Tammy acquires her own phallic substitute through Doyle's high-powered rifle (compounding the idea of a penis substitute is the fact the gun belonged to a tough and deeply masculine Marine) which she turns upon the dominating and violent father. By killing him, Tammy is physically and emotionally empowered for she has overthrown the power of the patriarch. Throwing down the rifle, Tammy is now in the position of masculine authority and so gathers her brother up in her arms and carries him out of the tunnel and into light.

As the film ends, Tammy and Andy finally manage to escape Britain in a military helicopter but the final images suggest the pandemic is far from over: the helicopter appears to have crashed in or near Paris and that Andy has continued the spread of the virus for the film concludes with a mass of the infected running out of the Metro towards the Eiffel Tower...

REFERENCES

28 Weeks Later (2007). Directed by Juan Carlos Fresnadillo [DVD], Europe: Fox International.

APPENDIX 2: *THE WICKER MAN (2006)*

The most significant difference between the original *Wicker Man* and Neil LaBute's remake (*The Wicker Man*, 2006) is the role reversal upon Summerisle: instead of the island being ruled by the patriarch Lord Summerisle it is instead controlled by a matriarch, Sister Summerisle (Ellen Burstyn). Critic Kim Newman suggests this shift of masculine power onto the feminine 'might have made sense with New Age or old hippie Wiccan trappings, but [instead] becomes an inverted *Stepford*, a ridiculous feminist dystopia' (2006: 83). Whilst Newman's comments are valuable in relation to analysing the remake it is possible to interpret this shift in power as an amplification of the subtler aspects of Hardy's original as the idea of the strong female was already evident within his version of Summerisle: of all the women seen within the film, the one who seems to represent the most stereotyped housewife, Mrs.. Morrison, in fact runs her own shop without the support of any male figure. Mr. Morrison is neither seen nor mentioned. It would therefore seem logical to extend this facet of representation in a more full blown manner, particularly in light of the continued progress of women's liberation. To this extent, LaBute renders all the women on Summerisle as powerful and all the men as weak and subordinate to them. This reinterpretation of social structure causes immediate friction with investigating police officer Malus (Nicholas Cage) who, throughout the film, tries to re-establish some sense of masculine control upon the island. These attempts culminate with him trying to galvanise a group of men into direct action against the matriarchs. The men listen to Malus and then simply turn away. On this Summerisle, the men clearly know their place.

As the narrative moves towards its sacrificial end, Malus, like Howie before him, steadily resorts to masculine actions in an effort to gain compliance from the islanders: unable to get Sister Rose (Molly Parker) to respond to his questions, he takes out his Officer's badge and shows it to both her and the class of children. He later draws his gun and demands information that way and, at the end, when the cruel plot is revealed to him, Malus again draws his gun and demands his freedom. The most alarming manifestation of Malus' masculinity is his vicious beating of Sister Beech (Diane Delano) and Sister Honey (LeeLee Sobieski) during which he punches the women in their faces and throats until knocked unconscious.

All of these incidents suggest that Malus perceives the social structure of Summerisle as a direct assault upon his masculinity. Unable to get the women to speak, respond or act in the way he wants, Malus quickly retreats behind established masculine symbols of authority, power and control – his gun and his badge. But what Malus fails to recognise is that those symbols carry little (if any) symbolic power on Summerisle. They do not form part of the islanders' symbolic language and, as a consequence, are rendered powerless by those who are confronted by them. The gun, however, does retain some of its potency as a weapon. As the narrative closes it is predictable that Malus will draw his gun but it is more predictable that the bullets will have been removed from its magazine. By removing the bullets the women of the island have once again impressed upon him their dominance for they have effectively castrated this phallic symbol.

These readings imply a further significant difference between LaBute's remake and the original for it has replaced the central religious conflict between Howie and Lord Summerisle with a sexist conflict between Malus and Sister Summerisle. Such is the extent of this conflict that the island's religious dimensions are used as a further means of attacking the matriarchal power structure: whereas Howie commented to Mrs.. Morrison that 'you're all mad' because of the rituals he has so far witnessed, Malus attempts to quickly impress his authority by telling Sister Summerisle that the island is not beyond the reach of the law of 'normal' society. Malus stresses 'normal', clearly indicating his perception of the island's religious structures. Ironically, this intolerance will, in part, make Malus the ideal candidate for the Wicker Man sacrifice – by being a stranger who has willingly come from outside into the community of Summerisle he has unknowingly made his contract with the very beliefs he is so quick to disrespect.

Whilst the agenda of sexual politics dominates the narrative and its potential critical interpretations, LaBute's remake can also be read within the context of a post-9/11 society: at its most basic, the story of The Wicker Man concerns an outsider authority figure entering into an alien location in order to deploy Law and Order to a specific situation. As they attempt to do this, both the indigenous people and the landscape become hostile, effectively attacking and consequentially killing this outsider. Parallels with the Gulf Conflict and the subsequent deployment of coalition forces within Iraq become evident quite quickly and suggest that the positive intentions of the outsider soon positions them as potential victim due to the very nature of the social and religious structures they are interacting with. Within the context of this reading, the narrative suggests that aggressive force is not a viable option and that working in sympathy with the people will result in the desired outcomes. While this seems a positive moral message to deliver, the contextual readings this constructs are not anti-American for it is all undermined by the concluding sacrifice: the pre-planned death of the authority figure suggests that the local people and their social order cannot be trusted, and so renders them as a social group capable of co-ordinated assaults and so strengthens the connection between the fictional narrative and real world events.

Such readings suggest alternate interpretations of 28 Weeks Later: within that narrative the US military are clearly positioned as an occupying force within the hostile territory of mainland England. Here, the military is the outsider who is confronted by the insurgent threat of the infected. Whilst non-confrontational efforts are made to contain the insurgency, the threat soon overwhelms and extreme actions are quickly and effectively put into place: a 'Code Red' is initiated by Brigadier General Stone (Idris Elba) which results in the termination of all hostiles and civilians.

Within this narrative construct, the US military is represented as a *positive* force whose good intentions are undermined by the insurgent threat. The military responds to violence with violence and terminates with extreme prejudice in an effort to ensure the total eradication of the virus. Whilst this may seem an aggressive mode of representation, it is counterbalanced by the film's adult protagonists, Scarlet and Doyle. As officers within the military, they construct an alternate representation between them through their attempt to ensure Tammy and Andy's safety. Whilst this is commendable, they have, like Malus, been deceived by the very people they are trying to help. As Douglas Rushkoff comments:

> '[Scarlet and Doyle] distinguish themselves and redeem our view of humanity through acts of self-sacrifice. It turns out, however, that they've sacrificed themselves on behalf of a child who carries the virus and goes on to infect the rest of the world. Humanity, like civil liberty, is no longer a strength but a liability. It's not a totally cynical or unpatriotic outlook: at least this Iraq war satire assumes America has the best of intentions.' (2007: 73)

REFERENCES

Newman, Kim. 'The Wicker Man', p. 83 in *Sight and Sound*, November 2006.

Rushkoff, Douglas. 'They walk amongst us or what I learned from watching zombie movies', pp. 72-3 in *Discover*, October 2007.

The Wicker Man (2006). Directed by Neil La Bute [DVD], Europe: Lionsgate.

CHRONOLOGY

DATE	NATIONAL EVENTS	UK CINEMATIC EVENTS	UK HORROR RELEASES
1970		Neil Marshall born 25 May.	Countess Dracula (Peter Sasdy) The Horror of Frankenstein (Jimmy Sangster) The House that Dripped Blood (Peter Duffell) The Scars of Dracula (Roy Ward Baker) Taste the Blood of Dracula (Peter Sasdy) The Vampire Lovers (Roy Ward Baker)
1971			Blood on Satan's Claw (Piers Haggard) I, Monster (Stephen Weeks) Lust for a Vampire (Jimmy Sangster) Vampire Circus (Robert Young)
1972			The Creeping Flesh (Freddie Francis) Death Line (Gary Sherman) Dracula AD 1972 (Alan Gibon) Frenzy (Alfred Hitchcock)
1973			Don't Look Now (Nicolas Roeg) The House of Whipcord (Peter Walker) Vault of Horror (Roy Ward Baker) The Wicker Man (Robin Hardy)

Year	Events	Films
1974	Edgar Wright born 18 April.	*The Beast Must Die* (Paul Annett) *Captain Kronos: Vampire Hunter* (Brian Clemens) *Frightmare* (Peter Walker) *The Legend of the Seven Golden Vampires* (Roy ward Baker) *Legend of the Werewolf* (Freddie Francis) *Madhouse* (Jim Clark) *The Satanic Rites of Dracula* (Alan Gibson)
1975	James Ferman becomes Director at the BBFC.	*The House of Mortal Sin* (Peter Walker) *The Shout* (Jerzy Skolimoxksi)
1978	'The Winter of Discontent': Trade Unions demand pay rises for their members and widespread strike action takes place across the UK, resulting in disruption of food, oil and petrol supplies as well as frequent power cuts.	
1979	Margaret Thatcher takes office as Prime Minister with the UK under a Conservative government. Handmade Films production company established by ex-Beatle George Harrison and partner Denis O'Brien.	*Alien* (Ridley Scott)
1980	Mary Whitehouse awarded a CBE for 'public service'.	*Inseminoid* (Norman J. Warren) *The Monster Club* (Roy Ward Baker)

1981	AIDS steadily enters the global consciousness.	Palace Pictures is formed by Stephen Woolley and Nik Powell with the intention to both produce film within the UK and distribute world cinema. They also open the Scala Cinema.	*An American Werewolf in London* (John Landis)
1982	The Falklands War begins on 2 April, ending on the 14 July.	The BBFC replace three of their certification labels: the A certificate becomes the PG certificate, the AA certificate becomes the 15 certificate and the X certificate becomes the 18 certificate. Film Four is established alongside the new terrestrial television channel Channel 4.	*Xtro* (Harry Bromley Davenport)
1983		Palace Pictures acquire the UK distribution rights to Sam Raimi's *The Evil Dead* and release it simultaneously theatrically and on video. Censorship campaigner Mary Whitehouse screens clips from *The Evil Dead* and various other 'video nasties' to MPs at the House of Commons. Director Raimi and Palace Pictures founder Nik Powell testify at Snaresbrook Crown Court regarding the distribution of Raimi's *The Evil Dead*. A verdict of Not Guilty is returned and consequential publicity ensures the film enters the video rental list at #1. Production begins on Palace Pictures flagship film, *The Company of Wolves*.	*The House of Long Shadows* (Peter Walker) *The Hunger* (Tony Scott)

Year			Films
1984		The 1984 Video Recordings Act introduced by the Conservative government, making it the first legislation specifically for the regulation of video. On 3 February David Hamilton Grant sentenced to 18 months in prison for the distribution of *Nightmare in a Damaged Brain* (Romano Scavolini, 1981).	*The Company of Wolves* (Neil Jordan)
1985	AIDS declared as a pandemic as it spreads across sub-Saharan Africa.	From 1 September all video recordings have to posses a BBFC Classification in accordance with the VRA.	*The Bride* (Franc Roddam) *Gothic* (Ken Russell) *Underworld* (George Pavlou)
1986		Publication of Clive Barker's first novel, *The Damnation Game*. First edition of *Samhain* magazine published.	*Rawhead Rex* (George Pavlou)

1987	On 19 August the Hungerford Massacre takes place: unemployed labourer Michael Ryan takes two semi-automatic rifles and a handgun and embarks on a shooting spree, killing 16 people and wounding 15 others before killing himself. Alongside the Dunblane Massacre in 1996, it remains one of the worst criminal firearms offences in British history. The tabloid newspapers claim Ryan was inspired by Ted Kotcheff's *First Blood* (1982) but it has since been established Ryan had never seen it.	Publication of Clive Barker's second novel, *Weaveworld*; and with the release of the author's directorial debut, *Hellraiser*, Pinhead, the first British horror icon since Dracula appears on screen.	*Hellraiser* (Clive Barker)
1988		First edition of *Fear* magazine published.	
1989			*Dream Demon* (Harley Cokliss) *Hellbound: Hellraiser 2* (Tony Randel) *The Lair of the White Worm* (Ken Russell) *Paperhouse* (Bernard Rose)

1990	Iraq invades Kuwait on 2 August. Margaret Thatcher resigns as leader of the Conservative Party and Prime Minister, shortly followed by the election of John Major as her successor on 28 November.	First edition of *The Dark Side* magazine published.	*Hardware* (Richard Stanley) *I Bought a Vampire Motorcycle* (Dick Campbell) *Nightbreed* (Clive Barker)
1992		Palace Pictures experiences financial hardship. After Polygram reneges on a deal to purchase, the Palace Group has to file for administration in May. First edition of *Shivers* magazine published.	*Dust Devil* (Richard Stanley)

1993	On 12 February, two-year-old James Bulger is abducted and murdered by two ten-year-old boys, Jon Venables and Robert Thompson near Walton, Merseyside. Both boys become the youngest people to be charged with murder in England during the twentieth century. The 'video nasty' moral panic is re-ignited when it is alleged that the boys had seen the film *Child's Play* (1988) on video. This was later definitively refuted by the investigating team, which did not stop the presiding judge from citing it in court.	Redemption Films founded with the aim of distributing and promoting European horror, sleaze and sex films in the UK. Scala Cinema closes down after the projectionist testifies against the management for illegal screenings of Kubrick's *A Clockwork Orange* (1971).	*Beyond Bedlam* (Vadim Jean)
1994	Tony Blair elected leader of the Labour Party and steadily establishes New Labour.	Peter Cushing, OBE dies on 11 August. Mary Whitehouse retires from President of National Viewers and Listeners Association.	*Interview with a Vampire* (Neil Jordan) *Mary Shelley's Frankenstein* (Kenneth Branagh)
1995			*Proteus* (Bob Keen)

1997	The Labour Party wins the General Election in a landslide victory, bringing an end to the 18 year leadership of the Conservatives and making Tony Blair the new Prime Minister. The global media are informed that the Roslin Institute has confirmed the first cloned animal, Dolly the Sheep, on 26th February and so instigating an international debate regarding the cloning of humans.	David Cronenberg's *Crash* wins the Special Jury Prize at Cannes. The BBFC later release the film uncut but is almost immediately banned by Westminster Council in London. Media hysteria reaches a peak with the film and its director publicly derided on the front pages of the national press.	*Darklands* (Julian Richards)
1998			*Razor Blade Smile* (Jake West)
1999		James Ferman retires as Director of the BBFC.	
2000		The UK Film Council established.	*The Bunker* (Rob Green)
2001	The 11 September terrorist attacks on the US.	Mary Whitehouse dies on 23 November.	*The Hole* (Nick Hamm) *Long Time Dead* (Marcus Adams)
2002		In July, Channel 4 announces the closure of Film Four as a result of failing to establish itself as a profit-making independent film company. James Ferman dies on 24 December.	*28 Days Later* (Danny Boyle) *Deathwatch* (Michael Bassett) *Dog Soldiers* (Neil Marshall) *My Little Eye* (Marc Evans) *Nine Lives* (Andrew Green)

Year	Notes	Films
2003		*The Last Horror Movie* (Julian Richards) *London Voodoo* (Robert Pratten)
2004		*Creep* (Christopher Smith) *Lie Still* (Sean Hogan) *Shaun of the Dead* (Edgar Wright)
2005	Twenty-year-old Tom Palmer murders two of his friends apparently after repeatedly watching *The Last Horror Movie*. UK distributor Tartan withdraws the film in 2007.	*The Descent* (Neil Marshall)
2006		*Severance* (Christopher Smith) *The Wicker Man* (Neil LaBute)
2007		*28 Weeks Later* (Juan Carlos Fresnadillo)
2008		*Doomsday* (Neil Marshall) *The Cottage* (Peter Andrew Williams)

BIBLIOGRAPHY

Barker, Clive. *The Hellbound Heart*, London: Fontana, 1991.

Barker, Clive. *Books of Blood: Volume 1–3*, London: Time Warner paperbacks, 1988.

Barker, Clive. *Books of Blood: Volume 4–6*, London: Time Warner paperbacks, 1988.

Benshoff, Harry M. *Monsters in the Closet: Homosexuality and the Horror Film*, Manchester: Manchester University Press, 1997.

Branagh, Kenneth. *Mary Shelley's Frankenstein – The Classic Tale of Terror Reborn on Film*, London: Pan Books, 1994.

Cartmell, Deborah, Hunter, I. Q., Kaye, Heidi and Whelehan, Imelda (eds) *Pulping Fictions*, Chicago: Pluto Press, 1996.

Chibnall, Steve and Petley, Julian (eds) *British Horror Cinema*, London: Routledge, 2002.

Clover, Caroline. *Men, Women and Chainsaws: Gender in the Modern Horror Film*, Princeton, NJ: Princeton University Press, 1992.

Creed, Barbara. *The Monstrous Feminine: Film, Feminism, Psychoanalysis*, London: Routledge, 1993.

Gelder, Ken. *Reading the Vampire*, London: Routledge, 1994.

Grant, Barry Keith (ed.) *The Dread of Difference*, Texas: University of Texas Press, 1996.

Goldberg, Ruth, *100 European Horror Films* (ed. Stephen Jay Schneider), London: British Film Institute, 2007.

Kane, Paul. *The Hellraiser Films and their Legacy*, Jefferson: McFarland and Co., 2007.

Hutchings, Peter. *Hammer and Beyond: The British Horror Film*, Manchester: Manchester University Press, 1993.

Le Blanc, Michelle and Odell, Colin. *Vampire Films*, Hertfordshire: Pocket Essentials, 2000.

Le Blanc, Michelle and Odell, Colin. *Horror Films*, Hertfordshire: Pocket Essentials, 2001.

Marriot, James and Newman, Kim. *Horror: The Definitive Guide to the Cinema of Fear*, London: André Deutsch, 2006.

McCarty, John. *Hammer Films*, Hertfordshire: Pocket Essentials, 2002.

Murphy, Robert (ed.) *The British Cinema Book* (second edition), London: British Film Institute, 2001

Newman, Kim. *Nightmare Movies: A Critical History of the Horror Movie from 1968*, London: Bloomsbury, 1988.

Newman, Kim (ed.) *The BFI Companion to Horror,* London: British Film Institute, 1996.

Paul, William. *Laughing Screaming – Modern Hollywood Horror and Comedy*, New York: Columbia University Press, 1994.

Pirie, David. *A Heritage of Horror: The English Gothic Cinema 194 –1972*, London: Gordon Fraser, 1973.

Pirie, David. *Vampire Cinema*, London: Hamlyn, 1977.

Punter, David and Byron, Glennis. *The Gothic*, London: Blackwell, 2003.

Rigby, Jonathan. *English Gothic: A Century of Horror Cinema*, London: Reynolds & Hearn Ltd., 2000.

Shelley, *Mary Wollstonecraft. Frankenstein*, London: Penguin Books, 2003.

Sheridan Le Fanu, Joseph. *In a Glass Darkly*, London: Wordsworth Editions, 1995.

Street, Sarah. *British National Cinema*, London: Routledge, 1997.

Tasker, Yvonne. *Spectacular Bodies: Gender, Genre and the Action Cinema*, London: Routledge, 1993.

FURTHER READING

Hammer

Hearn, Marcus & Barnes, Alan. *The Hammer Story: The Authorised History of Hammer Films,* London: Titan Books Ltd, second edition, 2007.

McKay, Sinclair. *A Thing of Unspeakable Horror: The History of Hammer Films*, London: Aurum Press Ltd, 2008.

Meikle, Denis. *A History of Horrors: The Rise and Fall of the House of Hammer*, Lanham: Scarecrow Press, 1996.

Specific Films

Barker, Clive, et al. *The Hellraiser Chronicles*, London: Titan Books Ltd., 2004.

Bradley, Doug. *Behind the Mask of the Horror Actor*, London: Titan Books Ltd., 2004.

Brown, Allan. *Inside the Wicker Man*, London: Sidgwick & Jackson Ltd, 2000.

Garland, Alex. *28 Days Later*, London: Faber and Faber, 2002.

Murray, Jonathan, et al (eds). *Constructing the Wicker Man: Film and Cultural Studies Perspectives*, Glasgow: University of Glasgow / Crichton Publications, 2005.

British Cinema: General

Allon, Yoram, et al (eds). *Contemporary British and Irish Film Directors*, London: Wallflower Press, 2001.

Barker, Martin, et al. *The Crash Controversy: Censorship Campaigns and Film Reception*, London: Wallflower Press, 2002.

Boot, Andrew. *Fragments of Fear: An Illustrated History of British Horror Movies*, London: Creation Books, second revised edition, 1999.

Murphy, Robert (ed.). *The British Cinema Book*, London: BFI Publishing, second revised edition, 2002.

Murphy, Robert (ed.). *British Cinema of the 90s*, London: BFI Publishing, 1999.

Sargeant, Amy. *British Cinema: A Critical and Interpretive History*, London: BFI Publishing, 2005.

INDEX OF FILM TITLES

STILLS INFORMATION

The publisher believes the following copyright information to be correct at the time of publication, but will be delighted to correct any errors brought to our attention in future editions.

Page 11 (*The Vampire Lovers*), Joel Finler Archive; pages 25 (*The Wicker Man*) and 39 (*Death Line*) BFI Stills, Posters and Designs; pages 49 (*An American Werewolf in London*), 79 (*Mary Shelley's Frankenstein*), 93 (*28 Days Later*), 125 (*Shaun of the Dead*) and 137 (*The Descent*) Aquarius Collection; page 65 (*Hellraiser*) Moviemarket; page 111 (*The Last Horror Movie*), Julian Richards/Prolific Films. All framegrabs within each chapter are taken from the respective Region 2 DVDs of the films.

BEYOND HAMMER